Mission O

A Story of Courage, Honor and Sacrifice

Written by A. J. Padgett with Frank Padgett

French Indochina - 1941

Mission over Indochine

Copyright 2012 by Arnold James Padgett

Cover design by A. J. Padgett

2012

Dedication

To my mother Sibyl Pharr Padgett and my grandmother Eva Masson Padgett. Both taught me the importance of keeping a sense of humor when the going gets tough. I wish I had listened to them more often and taken their advice.

Acknowledgements

I would like to thank the following people for their contributions to this book: My father Frank for his crackerjack memory, patience and time. It was a privilege working with him and one that very few sons ever get the chance to experience. My mother Sibyl, for the memories, anecdotes and yarns about family history. My wife Melanie who was there to read, edit and answer questions at 2 am. My sister Betsy, for all of her encouragement, her knowledge of family history and her excellent editing skills. My children Matt and Leianna, thanks for your encouragement, advice and belief in the project. Paul Ryan for your advice and encouragement. To Matthew, my brother for providing more family history. Thanks to Martin L. Mickelsen of Athens, GA, for his help and research material. Martin's information concerning the 308th Heavy Bomb Group and accounts of the Bobcat crewmembers, contributed greatly to this work.

Me kealoha ku'u home o Kaneohe

AUTHOR'S NOTE 7

PREFACE 11

CHAPTER ONE –A TOUGH ROW TO HOE.......................13

CHAPTER TWO – TRANSFORMATION 44

CHAPTER THREE - POWER UP 61

CHAPTER FOUR - JOURNEY TO WAR 69

CHAPTER FIVE –LULIANG BRIDGE CLUB.....................95

CHAPTER SIX – THE 13TH MISSION............................115

CHAPTER SEVEN – BAIL OUT 123

CHAPTER EIGHT - FRANK NEW YEAR'S DAY, 1945 127

CHAPTER NINE - BETRAYED 136

CHAPTER TEN - JOURNEY SOUTH 148

CHAPTER ELEVEN - FIGHT TO SURVIVE 155

CHAPTER TWELVE - FRENCH CAMP 174

CHAPTER THIRTEEN - BRITISH, DUTCH & AMERICAN
CAMP 203

CHAPTER FOURTEEN - FULL CIRCLE 221

EPILOGUE 233

AFTER THE WAR - A HISTORICAL PERSPECTIVE.......251

APPENDICES A – COMBAT REPORTS 254

APPENDICES B - WAR CRIMES TRIAL MANUSCRIPT 258

APPENDICES C - THE STORY OF ENSIGNS QUINN AND GRADY..**266**

APPENDICES D - OTTO SCHWARTZ STORY...................**268**

APPENDICES E - KOTOHIRA JINSHA NEWSPAPER STORY...**270**

PHOTO SOURCES...**271**

Author's Note

My father was a pilot during WWII, having flown bombing missions from a base in southern China. When I was young, he would tell us tales of his experiences during the Great Depression and going off to war. The stories I remembered most were the ones he told of the war. I knew many of them by heart and recall telling friends all about his adventures. Back then, boys my age were brought up on WWII movies, games and toys, spending hours shooting down airplanes, sinking battleships and playing with plastic toy soldiers. All of us wanted to be a soldier, sailor or pilot when we grew up.

As time passed, many of the stories of my father's experiences faded, replaced with my own. Then, in the mid 90's, there was a revival of interest around the country in World War Two and the men who had fought in it. It seemed the country was searching for the values those times represented, the selflessness, honesty and integrity that seemed to be disappearing from the new world order. World War Two had been a time of honor and sacrifice in America, as horrific deeds were countered by the courage and heroism of many young men, some mere boys, who went off to fight the Axis and gave it everything they had. The country had come together then as never before, united as one.

The renewed awareness of what some have called "The Greatest Generation" and the fact that its members were aging, made many realize that it was urgent that their stories be chronicled and saved for future generations. I thought of my father and his experiences during the war and decided that it was time to begin to record his story, for our family, as well as for others.

Unfortunately, right around that time, I began having health problems that affected my ability to write and I could no longer continue with the project. In 2003, I was diagnosed with ESLD (end stage liver disease). The years that followed were mostly a blur of hospitals and endless waiting. In 2009, I was told that a liver transplant was the only thing that could save my life. I was accepted as a liver transplant candidate by the University of California Liver Transplant Center in San Francisco and moved there to await a donor liver. By late October, my doctors gave me just days, possibly a week to live. Laying in the hospital, fighting to survive, I made a pact with myself that if I should make it through, I would finish this book. Maybe it was because writing it was a goal, something concrete and doable that I could shoot for. Or, maybe I saw some similarities in what was happening to me and what had happened to my father. I'm not sure.

On October 28, 2009, a liver was found and I went in to surgery that night. After nine hours of surgery, I was wheeled into intensive care with a new liver and life. In the months that followed, I began the journey back to health. I had to focus my awareness entirely on rebuilding myself, concentrating completely on coming back. It was tough and there were times when I thought I would never regain control over my life.

Eventually, my life became my own again. There was an easing of restrictions and medication. Gratitude replaced my fear that something would go wrong. I began feeling that I really was going to survive. I was on solid ground again.

By then, my father was in his mid eighties. I had lost so much writing time while I was sick, I knew I had better start hustling if I wanted to do what I had promised myself when I was laying in the hospital. It was time for me to get going and finish what I had started.

This is the story of my father and his remarkable generation. How they grew up in a hard pressed America, went off to war with the lucky ones returning to an America of new possibilities. It is a story of what happens when a country pulls together with a common goal, a lesson for this new age of dirty politics, machine gun consumerism and in your face television.

There are many men who, when called to service, unselfishly did what their country asked of them. My father answered the call bravely, putting his life on the line time after time, enduring extreme cruelty and deprivation with honor and humanity intact.

Preface

On the evening of December 31, 1944, a lone B-24 heavy bomber took off from a small, dusty airfield in southern China. Reaching their cruising altitude at 11,000 feet, the pilots set a southeasterly course and switched on the auto-pilot. Passing over the Hoang Lien Mountain Range at the eastern terminus of the Himalayas, then out over the Gulf of Tonkin, the eleven man crew settled in for the long and exhausting mission ahead. Shortly after takeoff, they experienced a small electrical glitch, but decided they could override the system and continue on with their mission. Their decision would have a profound impact on the fate of all aboard.

The plane the crew had nicknamed the "Bobcat", arrived in the CIB (China, India, Burma) theatre of war in September of 1944. Assigned to the 373rd Squadron, 308th Heavy Bomb Group operating out of Luliang China, the crew's orders were to find and destroy enemy shipping in the South China Sea using a new, top secret air to surface radar system. The men were well seasoned, having flown their aircraft half way around the world, from New York to their base of operations in southern China. They had since then flown over 120 combat hours on bombing missions over ground and naval targets.

On December 31, a Japanese naval convoy was sighted by allied submarines operating in the Gulf of Tonkin. That evening four aircraft, including the Bobcat, took off at half hour intervals on a mission to attack the convoy. According to Air Force post combat reports, the last radio message from the Bobcat was sent in the early morning hours of January 1, 1945.

The co-pilot was a 21 year old second lieutenant from Vincennes Indiana named Frank Padgett and this is his story.

Chapter One –A Tough Row to Hoe

"There were people living in old, rusted out car bodies.... There were people living in shacks made of orange crates. One family with a whole lot of kids was living in a piano box." *Anonymous, 1933*

Frank David Padgett, was born in Vincennes, Indiana on March 9th, 1923. Growing up between the boom years of the early twenties and the sudden economic bust of the Great Depression, he remembers the soup kitchens and bread lines and the huge number of people who were dispossessed because they had put their trust in a system they didn't understand. In the chaos that followed, many lost everything, finding themselves destitute and without hope.

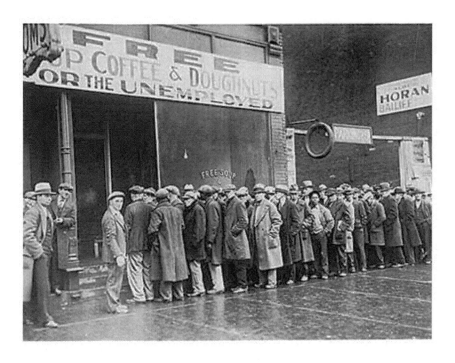

His mother and father were middle class folks and had a hard time trying to scrape by during those dark days. He, like many others of his generation, has carried the memories of those hard scrabble depression years with him throughout his life. His generation's shared experience of universal hard times seems to have strengthened their characters and toughened them up for the horrendous experiences and events that were to come just a few short years later, as mankind raced headlong towards the Second World War.

Frank's childhood was not easy. His parents did not get along well and constantly quarreled. They were both strong willed and often let their differences build up to the boiling point and beyond. The turmoil of living in a house with parents who were incapable of living together without constant conflict, created an atmosphere of instability that was very hard for an only child.

His mother was a legal secretary and homemaker who, for extra cash, played the piano for the silent movie houses in Vincennes. She was born Eva Masson in Pittsburgh, Pennsylvania in the year 1899, the daughter of a Belgian glass blower and his wife. When she was three years old, her father was offered a job in Italy and moved the family to Milan. They lived there until she was eight, when her mother and father, looking for new opportunities, decided to move back to America. Eva was happy where she was and didn't want to go. She was sure that moving would change her life completely. Everything she knew would be left behind, neighbors and friends, the family home, the culture, everything. But her reluctance to go was not a big consideration in her parents decision. They were only trying to do their best to survive the hard times.

In 1907, the Masson family moved back to America and settled in Vincennes, Indiana where they operated the North End Vincennes Glass Factory. Eva's inability to speak English immediately put her at a disadvantage in school. Her classmates teased and made fun of her incessantly and she found it very hard to make friends. She was a tough child and strong of will, but as the years rolled by she felt more and more isolated and alone. Eva was so miserable, that when she reached the eighth grade, her father pulled her out of school. He apprenticed her to a milliner with whom she worked until she was 16. She left the milliner job to study to become a legal secretary.

The world around her was rapidly changing as the old ways made way for the new. World War I had shaken the country with the horrors of trench warfare and poison gas. A large number of soldiers returned from the war afflicted with a new condition called "shell shock", the result of trauma to the nervous system caused by shock waves from high explosive artillery shells. It was a terrible war and America lost many of its finest, but there were some positive effects. The war had opened Americans' eyes to the larger world around them. Many young men came back from the war with more tolerant views toward the people and cultures of other countries.

It was a time of great change in America as new industries were born to manufacture the technological wonders of the day. In the cities, cars were replacing horses. Many homes now had electricity and some even had a refrigerator and a telephone. Radio was beginning to find its way into homes and movie theaters were opening up in towns and cities all over the country. America, having weathered the first world war and the flu epidemic of 1918, was fast becoming the richest nation on Earth.

Important social issues, impacting the lives of all Americans, were being argued in the legislatures, courts and in the streets. One of these was Prohibition. In 1919, the temperance movement prevailed with the ratification of the 18th Amendment making the prohibition of "intoxicating liquor" the law of the land. This divided the country over the question of whether one group should have the power to impose their values on another group by changing the Constitution.

The new law pitted non-drinking teetotalers against those who drank liquor. The law was ignored by most, as bootleg liquor filled the void left by the ban on legal liquor. Drinking clubs and "speakeasies" opened their doors, catering to the drinking public. This in turn ushered in the "Gangster era", as organized crime took over the production, sale and distribution of liquor in the United States. New economic powers grew and vast empires were built on the money that pored in to the coffers of those illegal enterprises.

In 1920, the women's suffrage movement gained a momentous victory with the passage of the 19th Amendment prohibiting the denial of voting rights based on the sex of any citizen of the United States.

It had taken over forty years for the proposed amendment to be ratified, making it part of the United States Constitution. The amendment, first drafted by Susan Anthony and Elizabeth Stanton in 1878, was opposed by many groups throughout the country, especially in the deep south. The enactment of the 19th Amendment permanently and profoundly changed the political landscape in America with women becoming a power to be reckoned with.

Eva's father was from the 'Old Country' and he was very strict. He kept a watchful eye on his only daughter and forbade her going out with young men. However, as a young woman coming of age in these turbulent times, she had different ideas. When she was twenty years old, she fell in love with an older man and married him without getting her father's blessing. When her father discovered this, he decided he had had enough of America. He sold his business and moved with his wife back to Belgium, leaving Eva alone with no familial support except for her husband and his family.

The man Eva married was a lawyer named David Padgett. His family had come from Kentucky in the early 1800's and moved into southern Indiana and Illinois. One branch of the family settled down in Vincennes, Indiana. David's father, A.J. Padgett, was also an attorney who had been admitted to the Indiana Bar in 1876. A.J.'s brother Charlie owned the Vincennes Grand Hotel and was well connected in the business community there. A.J. figured the town would be a good place to establish a law practice and moved there in the early 1900's.

In the late 19th century, lawyers traveled around, usually on horseback, to the different jurisdictions around the state. They were known as "Circuit Riders". By the early 20th Century things had changed. Towns had grown into cities and there were now trains and even some cars making everything more accessible. The telephone was becoming more common and lawyers no longer needed to jump on a horse to go and meet their clients. Most attorneys by then had settled down and built their practices in the towns where they lived. Despite these changes, there were still attorneys who worked the "Circuit", traveling around to rural courthouses representing clients in need of legal help. Usually, their clients were people of very modest means who paid for services with livestock, produce or anything that could be bartered. As a result, the "circuit riders" were often deep in debt and strapped for cash.

A.J. had been spared having to ride the "Circuit" and was able to set up his practice in Vincennes, where he prospered. His son David, followed his father into the business of law. David had gone to Georgetown and upon graduation, passed the Indiana bar exam and became a licensed attorney. Like many others in the trade, David drank heavily at times. He had a hot temper when intoxicated and had a reputation as a man who was quick to anger.

Early in his career, David worked as a prosecutor for Washington County in southern Indiana. One of the first cases he was assigned involved a robbery gone bad in which a store owner was gunned down and killed. One of the men charged in the case had been a high school classmate of David's. The trial proceeded quickly and when the sentence was handed down, the judge gave the defendant thirty years with no chance of parole. As he was led out of the courtroom in chains, he brushed past David and said "You bastard. I hope you remember me every night for the next 30 years. You hear?" This exchange hit David hard and he felt guilty that the man was going to prison. He started to drink even more and began backing away from the job. The drinking hurt his law practice and he found himself unable to keep up with the rigid court system that he dealt with daily. After a year or two, he completely stopped practicing as an attorney.

Shortly after David and Eva married, they purchased the "Peacock Coal Mine" in Wheatland, Indiana. The money came from Eva's mother, who returned to Indiana from Belgium just weeks before Frank's birth to help take care of him. David went into the mining business as an alternative to practicing law. The mine was just a small mom and pop operation. Eva kept the books and David, a jack of all trades, was the lead miner. He dug the coal, broke it up, bagged it and then trucked it to town to sell. They lived in a small house right outside of the mine with no running water, electricity or anything else. The mine and house were located at the top of a hill. Everyday, Frank's mother struggled up and down that hill, carrying the buckets of water they needed from a little stream in the valley below. Life was hard for them during that time and creature comforts were sorely lacking, except of course, the luxury of heat. They had a plentiful supply of their own coal to keep the house warm, a definite plus in the cold Indiana winters, but they had little else.

Padgett Family Picture 1928 - Frank in cap and striped socks.

The Twenties was an era of great economic growth and widespread prosperity, but there were sectors of the economy that were stagnant, especially farming and mining. The "Peacock Coal Mine" produced enough coal to keep their small family going, but it never paid off as David had hoped. In 1927, tired of digging coal, he decided to make another attempt at a law career. He took the Indiana Bar exam again and was admitted back into the fold. This time, he became a partner in A.J.'s firm and established his practice in Vincennes.

Due to the turmoil in their relationship, David and Eva separated many times. David did not spend a lot of time with his young son Frank, and at times, especially when he was drinking, he could be abusive to his family. As a young man, David was said to have been an athlete and good with his hands, but by the time Frank was born, the hard living had begun taking a toll on him. As Frank grew, his mother found it difficult to keep him in line. When he was three and a half, his grandmother Masson moved back to Belgium, leaving Eva to go it alone. As Frank grew older, Eva described him as shy, but difficult and opinionated. He was a child who had a mind of his own and wanted things his way.

At the age of five, he went to a street corner in his neighborhood, climbed on top of an old wooden crate he'd found, and made a speech exhorting people to vote for Al Smith, the Democratic presidential candidate in 1928. On another occasion, he stood up in class and described the reproductive cycle of chickens, including the rooster mounting the hen. His classmates were enthralled but not his teacher, who called home, telling Eva in graphic detail what Frank had done and suspending him for three days.

Frank had two half-brothers from his father's first marriage whom he greatly admired and looked up to. However, they were many years older and lived elsewhere in Indiana. Whenever his half-brothers came to visit, they would take him out for drives to go see friends and relatives. They would tell him stories of their exploits while they were growing up. One story was about the time Frank's half brother Bill was a young boy and had a bad fever. His temperature had skyrocketed and the doctor couldn't figure out what was wrong. His grandfather and uncle, dressed in their coats and ties, collected sheep dung from a nearby pasture, then came back home and brewed up some "sheep dip tea". It was a cure-all remedy passed down in the family from some unknown ancestor. They made Bill drink it and, lo and behold, it worked miraculously. In his memoirs, Bill said *"I have a mind's eye picture of these two well dressed gentlemen out in a pasture somewhere, gathering sheep droppings one by one. I can still smell the evil brew to this day. If they had told me it was "Indian medicine" or something like that, it would have been alright, instead, one of them told me what it was. Yes I drank it, what else could an eight year old boy do with two six foot tall, very determined men standing by his bedside."*

Frank's hometown of Vincennes, Indiana is located on the banks of the Wabash River in southwestern Indiana and is one of the oldest settlements west of the Appalachian Mountains. For thousands of years, different indigenous native tribes (mainly the Piankeshaw and Shawnee) had inhabited the area around Vincennes. French trappers were the first foreigners to settle there and it became a major center of the fur trade. The town was surrounded by fertile farmland and was connected to the Ohio River which made it very attractive to new European settlers. While Frank was growing up, its population was almost entirely white. It was a small Midwestern city just like many others located on the edge of America's breadbasket.

Frank attended public school in Vincennes and worked hard, getting good grades and making the most of what was offered. He started delivering newspapers in 1934 at the age of 11 and saved his money diligently. One of his customers was the neighborhood barber who was also a "holy roller" preacher. He would pay Frank extra to wake him up on Sunday mornings as he delivered the paper. The barber liked to have more than a few drinks after work on Saturday and needed something besides an alarm clock to get him up and out of bed so that he could deliver the good word to his congregation. The barber lived above his shop downtown, so Frank would ride down there early Sunday morning, get off his bike and bang on the his door to wake him up. Some mornings he actually had to go in the shop and up the stairs to shake the guy awake.

Frank was proud and excited to get his first paper route, even though it was on the rougher side of town. Although his customers were poor, they bought the newspaper, always wanting to know what their government was doing for them in the country they loved. In the days before radio and television, most people got their news from the newspapers. He liked being a part of a business that educated and informed the people.

The newspaper he worked for had a contest every year, the top prize being a trip to one of the big Midwestern cities. Frank was the Vincennes winner twice. The first time he went to Cincinnati, the second time to St. Louis. He was part of a group of around thirty carriers from all over Indiana. During the St. Louis trip, they stayed in a grand hotel, visited museums, galleries and a big amusement park. They also attended a major league baseball game featuring the New York Yankees against the St. Louis Browns. Before the game, the chaperones corralled all the carriers and took a picture of them with some of the players. The two Yankees on the left are Lou Gehrig and Joe DiMaggio. Frank is the tall blond kid in the second row standing to the right of the ladies with hats.

Like many young men of the time, Frank was a Boy Scout and enjoyed going out on excursions with his troop. He was interested in geology and spent time collecting unusual rocks, Indian arrowheads and artifacts that he found in the woods and fields around his hometown. When he was twelve, his grandfather gave him a 16 gauge shotgun and he and his friends hunted rabbits outside of town for sport and to put a little extra meat on the table.

Frank's mother and father were non-practicing Catholics so he had no formal religious training. As he got older, his unstable home life prompted Frank to start searching for some kind of anchor in his life. A woman in his neighborhood stopped him one day and asked if he had ever thought of joining the church. He said he had, so she told him to go to the church rectory and ask to speak with the priest. The priest began giving him instructions and in six months he was baptized. He came to see religion as a stabilizing force and refuge from his chaotic home life.

It was the summer of 1939, when at the age of 16 and having just finished his junior year in high school, Frank was bored and like teenagers everywhere, he was getting on his mother's nerves. Eva asked Frank if he had heard about the San Francisco World's Fair. He had, but never considered the possibility of going himself. She persisted, feeling it was high time to push him out of the nest and get him out of Vincennes to see the bigger world. Frank had never been that far away from home on his own before, but he mulled it over for awhile and decided maybe he was ready for an adventure. By the time he set off on the journey, as far as he was concerned, it had been his own idea from the start.

Frank's Aunt Arna and his Grandfather A.J. were now living in southern California and he wrote to them, asking if he could visit before going up to the fair in San Francisco. They responded yes, they would love to see him.

Aunt Arna and her family, including her father A.J., had settled in the town of Encino, north of Los Angeles. A.J. had always wanted to move west and had made various attempts to do so earlier in his life, but never found the right opportunity. Once, in 1890, he had packed up the family and moved to Salt Lake City. He bought a house and started a law practice there, but after about a year he ran afoul of the law, some said for gambling. The story was that he and another man had used a crooked "shoe", a box-like contraption used for dealing "Faro", a popular card game. In those days, cheating at cards was on a par with horse thieving in many parts of the west, and often a hanging offence. A.J. was forced to gather the family in the middle of the night and flee the city by train back to Vincennes. His gambling had gotten him into other dicey situations. One night in Vincennes, he stayed out too late in a saloon downtown. His wife Glen was angry and determined to teach her husband a lesson he wouldn't soon forget. She took her son David, Frank's father, into town, handed him her two pearl handled dueling pistols and ordered him to shoot out the windows of the offending saloon from a building across the street. David did what he was told and blasted out the windows of the saloon. This sent the patrons diving to the floor and crawling behind pool tables and the bar for cover. Fortunately, no one was hit and it did keep A.J. on the straight and narrow for awhile. After Glen died in 1935, A.J. finally realized his dream to move west permanently, going to live with his daughter Arna in Encino, California.

Grandmother Glen also had a rather remarkable life. She was the daughter of a Scottish plantation owner from Tennessee who had owned slaves. In 1850, he sold his plantation and moved to Washington, Indiana where he purchased a large tract of land, calling the farm 'Mount Aire'. He freed his slaves, built cabins for them to live in and hired them all as freemen. He farmed both wheat and corn and also mined coal. His daughter Glen, was born in 1855. When she was seven years old, she came down with "Spotted Fever", causing her to go deaf. She would tell anyone interested that the last thing she remembered hearing was the voices of the hired hands singing from their cabins on the farm. At times, her deafness provided a convenient excuse to ignore her husband. She would raise her newspaper in front of her at the breakfast table so that she couldn't see him. Other times, she would just close her eyes and pretend to be asleep if someone she didn't like was talking. People said she was "touched" because of her wild personality and penchant for riding her horse through town, chasing folks off the street.

Frank's Aunt Arna was another character by all accounts. She was Glen and A.J.'s second daughter and she no doubt inherited some of their wild and rowdy traits. She and one of her boyfriends had done some bootlegging in Vincennes during Prohibition, making beer for the local drinking clubs. One morning as she drove down Main Street, the load of beer she was carrying in the trunk of her car started leaking. Apparently her boyfriend had added too much sugar to the batch and the tops of the bottles began popping off. The cops, noticing her car was trailing some kind of liquid, pulled her over and amidst the continued bursting of bottles and the strong smell of beer, they arrested her. Her father bailed her out and admonished her to stop the foolishness, but to no avail. She married a vaudeville producer named Menlo Moore, who was from New York City. Besides producing shows, he was also a distributor of silent movies in the southern Indiana area. Unfortunately, Arna was a flirt and Menlo was a very jealous guy. This volatile combination turned into tragedy when Menlo shot and killed a traveling salesman in the Vincennes railway station for having an affair with Arna. He was thrown in jail, and while there awaiting trial, A.J. took on his case as his attorney.

Before going to trial, it was said that A.J. used some decidedly unethical means to win the case. The rumor was he had bribed some guards and arranged an unauthorized conjugal visit, secretly smuggling Arna into the jail to visit Menlo. When the trial finally started, she was seven months pregnant and the jury decided that a child must have a father and so they found Menlo innocent. After the baby was born, they packed up and moved to New York City. They settled there for a number of years and had two more children. Unfortunately, Menlo had a bad heart and died at a fairly young age leaving Arna and the children behind. They moved back to Vincennes where she had an affair with a priest from a nearby parish who was subsequently defrocked by the Catholic Church for his transgressions. His name was Ray and after his fall from grace, he married Arna and together with the children they headed for the greener pastures of California.

This was where Frank was heading on a bright summer day in 1939 as he began the first leg of his journey to the San Francisco World's Fair. He took the Greyhound to St. Louis where he transferred to another bus for the trip to Kansas City. In those days, some Greyhound buses were designed for long distance travel and had sleeper bunks in them. The buses were large and clean and a good way to travel if one had the time. From Kansas City, he took a sleeper bus heading west, falling asleep as they rolled across the flat farmland of middle America. When he awoke, the sun was just beginning to light the land outside. He realized they were climbing into the mountains of the Continental Divide. During the night they had crossed the Great Plains and were now in the foothills of the southern Rockies, heading onto the Colorado Plateau. When they pulled into Flagstaff Arizona, he got a room in a small motel, changed his clothes, then hopped on a bus to visit the Grand Canyon. Being a boy from the low hills of southern Indiana, traveling through the Rockies and seeing the Grand Canyon made quite an impression on him. Back home, a hill over 500 feet high was considered a mountain. Here, some of the mountains were over 12,000 feet high.

On the way back to Flagstaff, Frank purchased a few souvenirs from the Hopi Indians who had little stands along the road. They sold pottery, turquoise and woven baskets and he purchased several Hopi dolls for the folks at home. That evening, Frank met a middle aged couple in the lobby of his hotel. They noticed him because he was so young and without an adult traveling companion. They invited him to join them for dinner at a restaurant close to the hotel and he accepted. It turned out they were from Los Angeles and heading east to visit one of their children who lived in New Orleans. They were kind-hearted people and he appreciated their generosity. The next day, the bus traveled directly from Flagstaff, across the Mojave Desert and southern California, to the city of Los Angeles.

He was picked up at the bus terminal by his Aunt Arna and friends in a big, old Packard with a convertible top. As they left the city center, the land began to open up into nice rural countryside.

Encino, north of Los Angeles, was a very pleasant small town with lots of orange groves and small truck farms. The family compound, which they had named "Ranchero Mom Pa", was three acres of land with a large farmhouse and a smaller bungalow close by, surrounded with orange and walnut trees. It was quiet and so pretty that it all seemed a bit like paradise to Frank. His grandfather A.J. came out to greet him when they arrived. The old man was 84 years old now but still as spry as ever. Never one to let a game of cards pass him by, he played regularly with the crew that hung out at the house. Frank and his grandfather talked a lot while he was there and one of the highlights of their time together was a trip they all took to the beach at Malibu, where even A.J. went swimming. This was Frank's first experience swimming in the ocean. He swam out into the waves where some of the locals were "riding" the surf (body-surfing). He caught a wave himself, rode it in and was immediately hooked.

Aunt Arna had always attracted a certain crowd of people wherever she went. She loved parties and knew lots of movie actors and actresses, so life around the house was never dull. There were get-togethers on the verandah with people constantly coming and going. Several times a week, everyone staying there would pool their money and send Frank into town to place their bets on the horses. It was twenty miles to the race track at Hollywood Park, so he would ride down there with Whitey, his cousin Jimi's boyfriend. Whitey had played pro ball with the California Angels before semi-retiring and he now worked at the track. While Whitey was on the job, Frank would go and place the bets on the horses. It was all quite an eye-opener for a sixteen-year-old boy. Living with this eclectic group of part time actors and actresses, minor league sports figures and other Hollywood types was an education of sorts. He ended up staying there for close to a month before catching the bus up to San Francisco to stay with his father's oldest sister Marvel and her husband in Palo Alto.

Palo Alto is home to Stanford University and its tree lined avenues were nice and quiet compared to the traffic rush around the Fair and San Francisco itself. The 1939 World's Fair in San Francisco was an exposition of Pacific Rim countries and a celebration of the completion of both the San Francisco - Oakland Bay Bridge and the Golden Gate Bridge. The bridges were the engineering wonders of the time, giving testimony to the pride and work ethic of the American worker. The year was 1939. America had weathered the Great Depression and was now coming back, thanks to the jobs created by the WPA and other government programs.

The World's Fair was held on man-made Treasure Island, which is attached to Yerba Buena Island in the middle of San Francisco Bay. Yerba Buena Island is where the Oakland and San Francisco spans of the Bay Bridge join together. People could access the fair by car or bus, or they could take a ferry from different terminals around the Bay. Once visitors arrived at the Fair, there was a bus system that would transport them anywhere they wished to go around the fairgrounds.

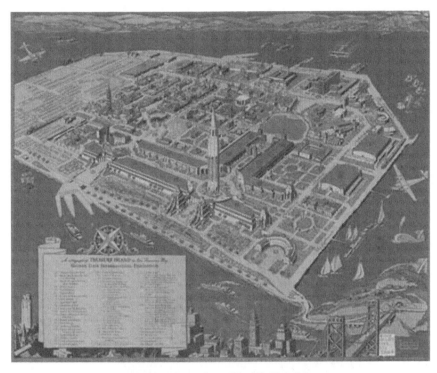

1939 San Francisco World's Fair Map

The Fair was a revelation for many who came, including Frank. There was little transoceanic travel back then, and the South Seas and Orient were considered very exotic. Few people had been there and most only knew what they had read in magazines or seen at the movies. The theme of the Fair was "Pageant of the Pacific" and primarily showcased the goods of nations bordering the Pacific Ocean. There were many elaborate exhibits by Pacific Rim countries such as China and Japan and even French Indochina.

Being a country boy from Indiana, Frank was intrigued by the exotic countries he had only read about.

The most exciting thing about the Fair for Frank was the chance to see the Big Bands, such as Benny Goodman, Glenn Miller and Duke Ellington, play at different venues around the mall. Frank went to see as many shows as he could. He also enjoyed the new foods available at the fair. His favorites were the "chip steak" sandwich and the "Pig in a Blanket". He kept going back to the restaurant stands that sold them over and over again. Something else that caught his interest was Bell Telephone Company's exhibition, where visitors could enter a drawing to win a free, three minute long distance phone call. Each contestant would be given a ping pong ball with a number painted on it. A wire basket rotating on a shaft was filled with the numbered ping pong balls. Every few minutes, the operator stopped the basket, reached in, pulled out a ball and called out the winning number. Frank entered the contest and won. He called home and talked to his parents for three minutes. That was a very big deal back then.

After a week of attending the fair, as well as seeing all the famous sights of San Francisco, Frank thanked his Aunt Marvel and saying goodbye, began the journey home. From San Francisco he boarded a bus to Reno where, while waiting for the next bus, he went into a casino and started playing the slot machines. All of a sudden the bells started ringing and out gushed a huge load of nickels. People began to gather around as he stuffed nickels into his pockets. It must have been a pretty big win because he soon found himself surrounded by the manager and casino bouncers. They checked his identification and when they found out he was only sixteen, they took all of his winnings and threw him out of the place. Disgruntled, he went back to the station and waited for the bus to Salt Lake City and got aboard, glad to be leaving.

Frank checked into a small hotel in Salt Lake City and rented a swimsuit, which at that time covered the entire body. Swimming in The Great Salt Lake felt strange, like he was floating on top of the water, not in it. He watched in amazement as a woman of exceptional girth walked slowly out into the shallows. Just as she reached the deeper water, she sort of sat down and rolled over onto her belly so that her rear end was bobbing out of the water. She floated there like a whale, except for the lack of a spout. All of a sudden, she began thrashing wildly. Someone, probably her husband, rushed out to her and rolled her back over so she could breathe. It was a lucky thing, too, because Frank had been too far away to help her in time and she might have drowned otherwise. From Salt Lake City, his adventure and vacation ended with a long bus trip directly home to Vincennes to begin his senior year of high school.

Frank did well during his senior year and got good grades. He graduated from high school in June of 1940 at the age of 17.

Before graduation, the principal spoke to the graduating class, exhorting them to continue their education and go on to college. At the same time, he subtly slipped in a "don't set your sights too high" message. After all, they were just country kids from a small Midwestern town and their chances of getting accepted to a prestigious college like Princeton, Harvard or Yale on a full scholarship were not great. Frank, who was never one to take the word of someone else without question, characteristically looked for a way to do it anyway. Having learned that the Harvard Club of Indiana was holding its yearly competition for a scholarship to the school, he applied for it. His mother drove him 60 miles down to Evansville, Indiana to take the required entrance test, which he passed, going on to win the scholarship. It was a tuition only scholarship, worth about $400 a year and it meant that he would be going to one of the top colleges in America. For a young man of modest means from a small mid-western town, this was a dream come true.

All other expenses would be Frank's responsibility and they included room and board, books and everything else he would need to survive the year. His parents, because of financial difficulties, could only help him out once in a while. He knew that it was going to be tough going. He had carefully saved up his newspaper delivery money over the years, but was going to have to live very frugally until he was lucky enough to find a job there.

In early September of 1940, Frank boarded a train from Terre Haute, Indiana and traveled to Cambridge, Massachusetts via Cleveland, Ohio and Albany, New York. The train was full of students, some were heading for school for the first time like himself, others were returning for another year. On the train, he met another student named Benji Hitts who was from Indianapolis. Benji had visited Harvard during the summer and seemed to know the ropes. He helped Frank find his way around during his first couple of days at Cambridge. After that, because of their different economic status, they went their separate ways. Frank, a scholarship student, was sent down to what he described as the "meat locker". Benji went to live in somewhat more posh environs on the other side of the campus. Once in a while they would bump into each other on campus, but they more or less went their separate ways because of their different circumstances and different majors.

Harvard Law School Building

As he entered Harvard in September of 1940, the winds of war were beginning to blow across the world. Germany had overrun much of Europe, the Battle of Britain had begun and the Japanese Army was steadily advancing through China and Southeast Asia. In October of 1940, draft registration began in the United States and the first draftees were inducted into the military. American colleges went on an accelerated schedule, classes were run all year long and included extra courses. Everyone knew that war was coming; it was just a matter of when.

Frank got along well with his classmates, but found himself weighed down by the academic intensity of it all. Coming from a small rural high school and being dropped into a highly prestigious college like Harvard was a huge change for him. Not only were the academic demands harder than he had expected, but surviving away from home was equally hard. He and all the other scholarship students were housed in an old, dilapidated dormitory that had little heat during the very cold New England winter. Many evenings he stayed in the heated library until it closed trying to keep warm, and many nights he slept in his overcoat because he didn't have enough blankets. He was dirt poor and struggling. He remembered that once, while sitting in his dormitory room, someone walked by eating a hot dog. He said that the smell wafting along in the cold air drove him nuts, he was so hungry but didn't have the money to buy one.

Frank's grades suffered that first year as he fought to catch up with the rest of the class. He missed home terribly, but his drive to succeed was strong and he persevered. He and a friend found jobs as waiters in one of the school dining halls, and they were able to get a free meal whenever they worked. Needing the free meals, he worked as often as he could, usually twice a day. That way, he was assured of at least one or two full meals every day. Things began to look up. Now he had a little extra spending money and was eating better and thus able to concentrate on his studies. His typical daily schedule was:

Work 6 am to 8am, Class 9 am & 10 am, Work 11:15 am to 1:45 pm, Class 2 pm to 5 pm, Work 5:30 pm to 7 pm. Then, study and homework until exhaustion took over.

By his second year, he had learned the ropes and was getting A's and B's. He joined the swim team and found that the camaraderie and competition opened up new avenues of social possibilities.

College man

In 1942, military recruiters from the different services came to the Cambridge campus, promising anyone who signed up with them would get a deferment and be able to finish college before being assigned to active duty. In May of 1942, Frank signed up with the Army/Air Force and was given a deferment. He was scheduled to graduate in June of 1944.

Everything finally seemed to be going his way. His grades were good, he had a job, a good social life and he was on the varsity swim team. His life began to resemble the ideal he held of what a Harvard student's life should be like. Everything he had worked so hard for was finally starting to happen.

Chapter Two – Transformation

There is a mysterious cycle in human events. To some generations much is given. Of other generations much is expected. This generation of Americans has a rendezvous with destiny. *Franklin Roosevelt, 1882 - 1945*

In the chapters that follow, different fonts are used to differentiate between Frank's first-hand account and other narration. **"Frank's personal account is in bold text and in quotations".** Other narration is in normal text style. *Reference materials are in italics.*

Frank's college life came to an abrupt end in February of 1943. He had recently become the number one breaststroker on the Harvard swimming team and was on a road trip to Brown University in Rhode Island with the team when his roommate called with the news that his orders to report for active duty had come in the mail. He was not quite 20 years old.

As the war continued to escalate, the armed services needed more men. The Allies were losing bomber pilots and crews at an incredible rate in both the European and Pacific theatres of war and they needed replacements. Harvard University had just sent Frank a letter giving him senior status, stating that he only needed to finish his current courses and pass final exams to graduate a year early. However, he was called to active duty before that could happen and wasn't able to graduate. He did not question the order calling him up, leaving Harvard without knowing what arrangements had been made by the university for his continued education should he return after his service commitment.

"On February 19, 1943, I reported to the Boston Armory for active duty in the U.S. Army/Air Force. For the next 13 months, I was trained as a pilot." Frank joined a large group of other men gathered at the armory near Copley Station. They were put on a train and sent to Atlantic City, New Jersey for basic training. It was bitterly cold on the train ride down. They hadn't been issued winter uniforms and all of them caught colds. Some even developed pneumonia and had to be sent to the hospital. During the following month, while stationed in Atlantic City, they did the usual military shuffle such as being sent out to guard empty buildings during the winter and other useful duty.

One day, Frank was told to report to the Chalfont Hotel to the sergeant in charge of the troops. This sergeant turned out to be a distant cousin from a hill town in south central Indiana.

He said to Frank, **"Your name's Padgett?"**

"Yes sergeant."

"Well you and me is cousins, and I like to take care of kin. I'm going to give you a little advice about getting by in the Army.

Yesterday I noticed that you and your buddies finished moving chairs and tables around at the armory early and you came back and then got assigned to do another job."

"Yes sergeant." said Frank.

"Well no one here's looking for high achievers. You just need to do your job and keep your head down and you'll get along just fine".

The sergeant assigned Frank to a cushy job doing guard duty at night in an armory on a quiet side of town. The building was heated, so as soon as he got there he would go inside, fold out a cot and sleep until he was relieved in the morning. He would then go to morning chow and start day duty well rested. Frank, being left handed, had always had trouble with directions, as in right or left, and this became problematic almost immediately during marching drills at Atlantic City. His solution was simple. He picked a pebble off the ground and kept it in his right hand for a week or so until he no longer needed it.

After a month in Atlantic City, Frank and a group of other recruits were put on a train to State College, Pennsylvania to take some of the courses necessary for air duty. The courses included gunnery practice, oxygen indoctrination, a ground phase of flight training (aircraft identification, code and maps, charts, and aerial photos), meteorology, trigonometry, aircraft recognition and basic information about radar systems. They had their first taste of flying in Piper Cubs and accrued their first ten hours of airtime. They were there for five weeks and stayed in fraternity houses that the Air Force had taken over. This was during the normal school year and many of the male students had already been drafted, so there were a lot of friendly female students about. It was a very good time to be a single young man and a flyer at that.

Becoming an Army/Air Force pilot during WWII was not easy, simple or quick. Consider that 324,647 cadets entered training between January 1941 and August 1945. 132,993 washed out or were killed during training. This attrition rate of nearly 40%, was due primarily to physical problems, accidents or inability to master the rigorous academic requirements. The training process involved several phases, and the cadet could "wash out" anywhere along the line.

From State College Pennsylvania, they took a train to Nashville for specialty classification. Here, they were given a series of tests to measure skills, psychological aptitudes, interest, knowledge, physical qualifications, and other characteristics. By weighing different sections of the psychomotor and psychological examinations, officials hoped to be able to determine a relative aptitude score, or stanine (standard nine) for pilots, navigators, and bombardiers. Army officials began using the term stanine in 1942.

It represented a score on a standard scale of measurement, which ran from 1 (the lowest) to 9 (the highest). Classification personnel used these stanine scores as a common index to place trainees in the proper training.

Besides the psychological testing, they drilled, did calisthenics and were given a battery of physical tests. Mostly they just hung around, bored and waiting to be classified as a pilot, navigator or engineer. Frank had originally signed up to be a navigator. He was fairly sure that he would automatically be disqualified as a pilot because he was left handed. To his surprise, after a month of waiting, he was classified as a pilot, assigned to a group of other pilots in training and sent to the next posting.

Before Frank left Nashville, his parents drove down from Vincennes one weekend to see him. They took him out for a chicken dinner in town - a real "Southern" style chicken dinner with all the trimmings. His dinner cost $1.50 and included a huge slab of peach pie and ice cream. The name of the restaurant was the Maxwell House and it served a locally popular blend of coffee that Teddy Roosevelt supposedly said was "good to the last drop" and went on to become the national brand still around today. This dinner was definitely the highlight of his time spent in Tennessee.

The next posting was Maxwell Field outside of Montgomery, Alabama for pre-flight training. It was summer and hot, down south type hot, where you sweat in the shade.

"It was early July and miserably hot and we were made to double-time everywhere we went. Everyone came down with heat rash. We each had two sets of coveralls which quickly became sweat soaked. I'd wear one pair all day, then rinse them out in the shower and hang them to dry. Unfortunately, the high humidity kept them from ever getting dry, so on the second day, I would put on the damp pair because it hadn't had a chance to dry yet. Constantly wearing wet clothes caused a terrible skin rash, so I'd throw a handful of Calamine powder on the bed sheets at night, but the rash never went away."

Maxwell Field was a typical military boot camp. The new recruits were required to double time everywhere, drilled incessantly, had early curfew, cold showers and hazing. Fortunately, the hazing was stopped after about a week when the camp commander decided to abolish the class system which permitted second month students to harass first month students. That ended the old "Drop down and give me 20" in the blazing hot sun.

One day, the camp commander decided to have a 5 mile race. The losing man would be assigned to overnight guard duty for a week, 10 pm to 7 am. Frank had been a swimmer, not a runner, and he was sure he would have a hard time keeping up with the leaders.

He looked around and spotted a chap who looked like he might have been a cross-country runner and when the race started, Frank got in position in back of the guy and drafted behind him during the race. Sure enough, he finished in a respectable position. Frank was learning to use his smarts the way his cousin in Atlantic City had told him to.

His body a bit fitter, Frank was shipped off to Cape Girardeau, Missouri for primary flight school to begin the slow, arduous work of learning how to fly an airplane. At that time, recruits had no idea what type of aircraft they would be assigned to, and being young men, most of them wanted to be fighter pilots. In Frank's case, at 6'-2", his height more or less automatically excluded him from flying fighters, their cramped cockpits being too small for his long legs.

Between February 1942 and March 1944, the three regional classification centers processed 400,000 aircrew candidates: 260,000 (65 percent) as pilots, 40,000 (10 percent) as navigators, and 40,000 (10 percent) as bombardiers. The remaining 60,000 (15 percent) were eliminated for various reasons: physical disability, low aptitude, etc.

The fact of the matter was that the Army/Air Force was losing bomber pilots and crews faster than any others and it needed to fill the ranks back quickly. At that time, they were pumping young men through flight training at an incredible rate. Approximately 27,000 heavy bombardment crews were trained in the period between December 1942 to August 1945. The attrition rate for flyers in training was so high, they had no choice but to hustle the recruits through flight school and hope for the best.

Flight instructors were literally dropping recruits into trainer cockpits first thing, putting them in the air before they had time to get their bunk assignments. Instructors wanted to "wash out" the unsuitable candidates with the least unnecessary loss of airmen, instructors or aircraft. Initially, a flight instructor usually flew alongside the recruit and had his own set of controls and could take over in the event the recruit got into trouble. Unfortunately, once the instructor determined the recruit was ready to fly alone, mistakes still happened. For young men totally unfamiliar with a machine that flies, this sometimes ended in disaster.

Training losses were high with over 35,000 recruits killed in non-combat deaths. Nearly 40% of all accidents occurred during landing. Second in importance were accidents which took place in flight and accounted for approximately 29% of the total. 16.1% were taxiing accidents and 11.5% occurred during take-off.

Young men who made it through basic training faced even longer odds when they started flying combat missions. The United States Army Air Forces incurred 12% of the Army's 936,000 battle casualties in World War II. Only the Army Ground Forces suffered more battle deaths. Total USAAF combat casualties were roughly

65,000. Of these, 45,000 were listed as KIA (killed in action), 3,640 died of wounds and 3,603 were missing in action and declared dead. 41,057 USAAF men became prisoners-of-war. Another 63,000 were listed as other-battle casualties.

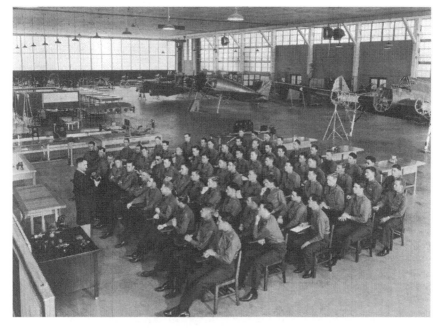

Cadets in Class

Recruits trained in a single engine monoplane named the PT 23 which had to be hand cranked to start the engine. It was the most basic type of trainer with two throttle settings and non-retractable landing gear. The plane had a rear wheel that could rotate 360 degrees and the pilot pushed on the brake pedals to control the front two wheels to steer the plane while on the ground.

PT-23 Trainer

Frank soloed in 6 hours without any problems which was considered outstanding.

"The field at Girardeau was grass and extra long, so all you did was point the airplane down the runway and push the throttles to full power. As you gathered speed, you could feel the plane respond to the controls. When you reached takeoff speed, you slowly pulled back on the main control stick and the nose of the plane began to lift. If there was a crosswind, you counteracted the force of the wind with your foot pedals. You had to be careful though, because pulling the stick back too far could cause you to go into a stall. Likewise, pushing on the pedals too far one way or the other could cause the plane to

turn too fast. You might find yourself looking at your tail out of the side window."

After two months at Cape Girardeau, Frank was sent on to Malden Field in Missouri for training in another single engine aircraft named the BT 13. It was a little more sophisticated than the PT-23 with a enclosed cockpit and retractable landing gear.

BT-13 Trainer

The recruits got another 65 hours of flying time at Malden before they were sent to Stuttgart, Arkansas for advanced training in the twin engine AT-10. Besides having two engines, the AT-10 had variable pitch propellers and retractable landing gear, the next rung up the ladder to flying large, four engine bombers.

AT-10 Trainer

The only time he had any trouble during advanced training was when he was flying with an instructor at night, learning to land on instruments only. As he came in on his first pass, a 50-mph. crosswind bounced them so hard that for a second he thought they had crashed. The episode really shook him up and he was sure that he was going to wash out. But the flight instructor was a professional and a good guy who told him to calm down and try again. On the next pass he landed without mishap.

During the time between primary through advanced training, one of Frank's fellow recruits became an "Ace", meaning he had brought down five planes. During primary training, the guy misjudged his approach and came down short, landing on two other planes and wrecking all three. Then, in basic, he hit some turbulence on landing and flipped his plane over on the tarmac. Finally, in advanced training, his landing gear wouldn't come down and he had to do a belly landing, wrecking the plane. That made five planes, hence the "Ace" designation by the rest of his classmates.

By the time air crew and combat crew members reached the crew training base they had many months of training in the techniques and skills that made pilots, navigator, bombardiers, flight engineers, radio operators, and gunners. OTU/RTU training put these highly trained individuals into a heavy bomber, polished each man until he was a master of his specialty, and melded the individual specialists into a "Combat Team".

Frank graduated from Flight School in March of 1944, got his wings and was appointed a Second Lieutenant in the United States Army/Air Force (USAAF). He was sent to Westover Field outside of Springfield, Massachusetts as a co-pilot for Aircrew Transition Training. This was the first time that he and his crew came together as one.

Bobcat Crew at Westover Field - Frank front row kneeling - far right

The type of aircraft they were assigned to was the B-24 "Liberator". It was a large, four engine heavy bomber, the backbone of the allied bombing fleet in the Pacific as well as in Europe. Being a four engine aircraft, the B-24's main controls were spread out, making it easier to fly, even for a 'lefty' like Frank.

While going through training at Westover, Frank ran into Benji Hitts, who he hadn't seen since Harvard. They decided to have a drink at a local bar and look for Smith College girls. Smith, which is located in Westover, was an all women's college. While they were sitting in the bar having a drink, a good-looking girl came up to them and asked if Frank and Benji would like to go to a dance over at the college. "Of course" they both blurted at once. As they were walking over to the campus, a bus full of infantry soldiers went by on the way to being dropped off in town on leave. Frank flagged down the bus and invited all of the soldiers, including the driver, to the dance. It turned out that they were on their way overseas the next day, and getting to go to a dance, especially at an all women's college was just about the best thing that could have happened to them. Frank later said that the war created a kind of camaraderie that made people think about each other more often and consider doing things they would not have done otherwise.

From Westover, Frank's next stop was Langley Field, Virginia for intensive low altitude bombardment training using a newly developed radar system named LAB, which stood for Low Altitude Bombing.

Langley Field, Virginia

It was essential that each crew member understand their responsibilities for their particular jobs, and also to each other. They were required to complete sustained high-altitude flights, evasion exercises, and precision bombing runs. Units had to demonstrate their ability to take off, assemble and land together; to operate in the air under radio silence and through overcast skies; to fly all types of formations; and to execute simulated bombardment missions.

Langley field was a good location for this sort of training because the waterways surrounding the base allowed them to set decoys and practice low altitude bombing runs that simulated a combat run. The crew was there for over four months, learning to fly a B-24 and use the new radar system installed on their aircraft.

Chapter Three - Power Up

"The United States is like giant boiler. Once the fire is lighted under it, there is no limit to the power it can generate." *Winston Churchill*

The B-24 "Liberator" gained a distinguished war record with its operations in the European, Pacific, African and Middle Eastern theaters. Over 18,000 of them were built during World War Two. Winston Churchill used one as his personal transport aircraft. From the start, the B-24 was cleared for a loaded weight of 56,000 lbs and by mid-1942, it was operating at 60,000 lbs, making it the heaviest aircraft in production in the USA. Plans were rushed ahead for production on a scale never before seen. The San Diego plant had already been nearly tripled in size. A vast new factory was built in 1941 outside Fort Worth, Texas, with a main hall 4,000-ft long and 320 ft wide. In 1941, the largest factory in the United States had been built by the Ford Motor Co. at Willow Run, near Detroit. By August 1942 Willow Run was on line, producing 200 complete bombers each month, plus 150 sets of parts for other assembly lines.

The B-24J was a modern, impressive bomber with a deep and husky fuselage and very large, oval fins and rudders. Chunky and bristling with guns, rather than beautiful and streamlined, it was functional and able to carry a large payload. It was a complicated and advanced machine, leading to prolonged pilot training programs and on occasion to severe attrition. Even for a pilot fully qualified on this type of aircraft, it was demanding to fly. It was eventually cleared to operate at such high weights that some take-offs became marginal even with full power on all engines.

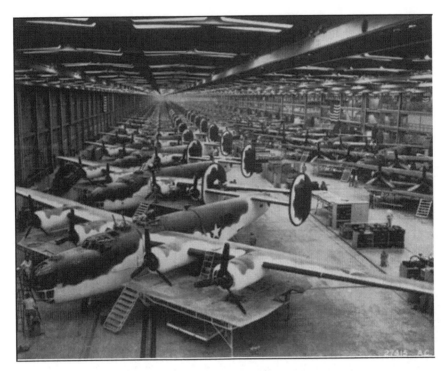

B-24 Production Line

Flight stability was also marginal, and escape from a stricken machine was extremely difficult once the pilot or pilots had let go of the controls. It tended to spiral down making escape almost impossible. Many B-24 crew members were hit by the tails or the tail plane when bailing out, killing them instantly.

For armament, the B-24 carried twin turret mounted .50-cal. Browning machine guns in the nose, upper and lower ball, waist, and tail turrets, a total of 10 heavy machine guns. The plane had a top speed of 290 mph; wingspan was 110 feet; fuselage length, 67 feet; height, 18 feet. It had a range of 2,100 miles and could carry a bomb load of between 1,200 to 8,000 lbs, depending on the range of mission. The service ceiling for the B-24J was 28,000 feet.

B-24 Liberator Bolivar

Besides being a bomber, B-24's were used as heavy lifters, carrying supplies and ammunition to forward bases. They could also be fitted out as gasoline tankers, able to carry 2,900 US gallons of fuel in metal tanks built into the fuselage. Sometimes, they used rubber bladders that could be taken out of the plane when they got to their destination, although these were not used very often. All B-24's were equipped with an inert-gas fire suppression system.

The B24 had a catwalk down the center to provide structural strength and also provide crew access to the rear fuselage. To enter the aircraft, one had to flick a small hydraulic lever on the right side of the bay. This opened the bomb doors, which rolled up the outside of the fuselage similar to a roll-top desk, the moving sections driven by large sprockets working directly on the corrugated inner stiffening skins. The crew of eleven climbed up onto the catwalk, the pilots, navigator, bombardier, radar operator, ball turret gunners and radio operator going forward while the waist and rear turret gunners went aft.

There were some shortcomings in combat with the B-24 as well as the B-17. Primarily, they were vulnerable to head-on attack. The internal protection was so poor that in Europe and the Pacific, numerous bombardiers, nose gunners and pilots were killed by shells entering through the aircraft's nose, and many aircraft were lost due to catastrophic hits to the nose. Some pilots took to carrying slabs of sheet armor held by hand in front of their bodies during crucial periods. In later models, the nose armor was beefed up to give more protection, but as with most things on an aircraft, adding weight had to be balanced by subtracting weight somewhere else.

B-17 Damaged by Anti-Aircraft Fire

In late 1942, the Army/Air Force began development of a new radar system that could detect surface shipping from long distances. This new radar assembly was top secret and crews working with it were forbidden to talk to anyone about it. In 1943, a number of B-24's were outfitted with the newly developed radar system nicknamed 'LAB' radar and it was integrated with the Norden bombsight. The planes, part of the Third Sea Search Squadron out of Langley Field, Virginia, were used to develop and test the system. The LAB system (Low Altitude Bombing) gave the bombardier a precision targeting system that allowed the bomb load to be dropped on enemy shipping at night with a very high degree of accuracy without having to make actual eye contact with the target. These new night flying, radar guided B-24's were the first electronically guided aircraft used by the U.S. military.

It was decided that the LAB equipped bombers could be a key factor in disrupting the flow of oil and other essentials in and out of the South China Sea. Japan counted on all of this material, especially the oil, to continue fighting. In 1943, a group of ten LAB equipped B-24s was sent to the South Pacific to aid in the Pacific Islands campaign. They proved to be incredibly effective and in early 1944, the first waves of similarly equipped B-24J's, the latest model, were flown across the globe to a couple of airfields in Southern China, joining General Claire Chennault's 14th Air Force. The B-24J's of the 308th Heavy Bomb Group began flying missions over the Gulf of Tonkin and were extremely successful at sinking enemy shipping, as they had been in the Pacific Islands.

B-24 LAB Bomber

However, there were some very large drawbacks for crews flying LAB radar guided bombing missions. These missions were always flown at night and they required pilots to drop down under 1000 feet when making their bomb runs. This subjected them to intense enemy anti-aircraft fire as they approached their targets and as they were flying away. These missions were some of the most dangerous of the war, and casualties were high. Men in the nose and the ball turret positions were particularly vulnerable as they were only protected by the Plexiglas windows surrounding them.

Because of the secrecy surrounding the LAB project and the missions flown by the 308th Heavy Bomb group, information about these men and their mission did not become public knowledge until well after the war was over.

Most Americans knew little or nothing about the CIB (China, India, Burma) theatre of war during WWII. Most of the press coverage was of the big battles fought in Europe and the Pacific. The backwaters of China, Burma, India and French Indochina were never in the spotlight. Many brave men lost their lives on these far off battlegrounds, unknown to most Americans. They fought and died under terrible conditions with little help from the outside. Their hard work and courage helped to win the war against Japan.

The Death of the Ball
Turret Gunner
by Randall Jarrell

From my mother's sleep I fell into the State,

And I hunched in its belly till my wet fur froze.

Six miles from earth, loosed from the dream of life,

I woke to black flak and the nightmare fighters.

When I died they washed me out of the turret with a hose.

B-24 Ball Turret Hit by Enemy Fire

Chapter Four - Journey to War

"I fear we have awakened a sleeping giant and filled him with a terrible resolve"
Admiral Isoroku Yamamoto

In September, 1944 Frank and his crewmates were sent to Mitchell Field on Long Island to pick up their plane, a B-24 Liberator, the latest in the series. As they walked out on the field, the airmen were excited when they caught sight of their brand new plane. It had no paint yet and its shiny aluminum skin shone in the midday sun. This was one of the newest versions of the B-24, the "J" series, and was equipped with the most advanced LAB radar unit and Norden bombsight. They nicknamed their new plane the "Bobcat". They began break-in flights, training with the new systems and getting used to the aircraft.

In October of 1944, with their training over, Frank and his fellow crewmen began their journey across the world. The trip would take them over two weeks and cover more than 12,000 miles before reaching their final destination. The names of the young crewmen who had so recently been taught how to fly and were now assigned to fly this giant four-engine bomber to war, were:

Pilot	Robert W. Smith, Lieut.
Co-Pilot	Frank. D. Padgett, Lieut.
Navigator	Everett A. Clark, Lieut.

Bombardier	Harry W. Sherer, Lieut.
Radio Operator	Stanley J. Brach, Sgt.
Radar Operator	Joseph P. Medon, Staff Sgt.
Engineer	William Gottschall, Sgt.
Nose Gunner	Hugh C. Pope, Staff Sgt.
Top Turret Gunner	George Uhrine, Sgt.
Ball Turret Gunner	John J. Webster, Cpl.
Tail Gunner	Will D. Sanderson, Staff Sgt.

"We were excited. As a young man, the thought of going to war was enough to get any red-blooded kid's heart racing. We were going off to defend our country against the Axis. We didn't really think about the danger. We were all thinking about the adventure and what was ahead. We were young and invincible".

Picture of Crew at Mitchell Field
Frank back row standing – second from right

At Mitchell Field on Long Island, they were briefed on their mission. They were to fly up to Bangor, Maine, and then on to Goose Bay, Nova Scotia. They were given a sealed envelope containing further instructions but were told not to open it under any circumstances until they had taken off from Goose Bay. The plane's autopilot had stopped working just prior to taking off from Mitchell Field. There was no time to fix it there, so they had to fly the plane manually for the duration of the trip.

Before taking off from Bangor, the plane was loaded up with a very large amount of provisions, packed in removable bins in the bomb bay. They were also given fleece lined flight suits by the ground crew. They were very thankful for these as the weather was freezing and they were heading north to Newfoundland. When they landed at Goose Bay, it was a lot colder. They spent two days there while their plane was serviced, loaded again with cargo and topped off with fuel. Goose Bay was crowded with many B-24's on their way to the 15th Air Force in Africa and Italy, and to the 10th Air Force in India. There were also many transport aircraft taking supplies to Africa and Southern Europe.

Waiting for Takeoff

They got into line for takeoff with everybody else and waited their turn. Planes were taking off every three minutes but because there were so many, their plane wasn't cleared for takeoff until 1 a.m. in the morning.

"Smitty asked me if I had ever taken off in a fully-loaded B-24. I hadn't, but neither had he. So he said to me, 'You do it.' I

said okay and shoved the four throttles forward and we began our roll. As soon as we were airborne, and just a trifle over stalling speed, we lost all vision."

"I dropped my seat down to its lowest level and flew on instruments until we climbed out of it."

The visibility was down to 200 feet because of the smoke from a large peat bog fire. Added to this was the fact that many residents of Goose Bay burned peat to heat their homes. There was a local inversion layer keeping it from dissipating, so visibility was practically down to zero.

Because of his instrument training, Frank knew what he needed to do. It takes a lot of training and nerve for pilots to drop their seats down so that they can no longer see the horizon, lock their eyes to their instruments and have the faith that the instruments are giving them the right information. He did what he had been trained to do and off they went.

The concept of flying an airplane using only instruments goes something like this. Imagine driving a car at night. Suddenly the headlights go out. It's pitch black, there is nothing out there to see, it's just black. Equilibrium is lost and the roadway is no longer visible. The only option is to hit the brakes and stop the car. Fortunately, instrumentation had been developed by that time to help guide pilots in any low visibility situation. The main instruments were the altimeter, which tells how high you are; the Artificial Horizon that shows the aircraft's attitude relative to the horizon, the Turn and Bank Indicator that shows the rate of turn and the Airspeed Indicator that shows the aircraft's speed. If a person has learned how to read the instruments correctly, they can give a complete picture of the aircraft's relationship to the world around it, especially the ground below.

Eyes on the Instruments

When they reached cruising altitude in formation, Frank and Smitty opened the Manila envelope with their orders. Their final destination was a small airbase in southern China. From Goose Bay Newfoundland, they were to fly to Terceira in The Azores,

74

then on to Marrakech in Morocco, Tunisia, Cairo in Egypt and Abbadan in Iran. From Iran they flew on to Karachi, up to Agra and then across the sub-continent to Chabua, a city on the Brahmaputra River in eastern India. Finally, they flew over the Himalayan Mountains to their final destination, the small city of Luliang in Yunnan Province in southern China.

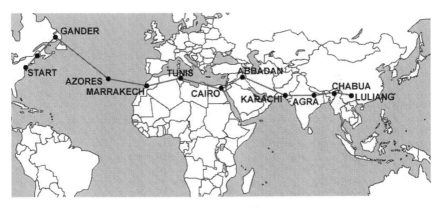

The Route to China

The Azores are close to the equator, about two thirds of the way to Africa. Smitty told the crew, none of whom had ever been overseas that they were heading for the tropics. Everyone was all smiles and looking forward to getting out of the cold. Heading down to warmer weather sounded really good to them. The further they traveled south, though, the warmer it got and they were sweating buckets because of the fur lined flight suits.

The flight across the Atlantic could be dicey because of the extreme range and limited fuel capacity. Before leaving, they had been briefed about watching their fuel consumption. It required a judicious hand to adjust the fuel to air mixture, as too little fuel overheats, with too much you run out of fuel and have to ditch in the ocean. The B-24 was not easy to trim for optimal fuel consumption, so the pilots had to stay alert as the weight in the aircraft shifted as fuel was consumed. It took them 8 hours of flying before landing on the steel mesh runway in Terceira. There was a huge bang when they touched down because they were still heavy with the fuel they had saved. The steel mesh sheets that formed the runway were interlocking but they still made an incredible racket whenever a plane landed.

"We hit the ground with huge bang. For a moment we thought our landing gear had collapsed".

The first thing they all did once they had landed and secured their ship, was to peel off the fleece suits, take a cold shower and change into their regular warm weather flight suits.

The Azores were governed by the Portuguese and had been for many hundreds of years, dating back to the 13th century. The islands had been a main waypoint for sailing ships engaged in the Far East spice trade as well as trade with the New World. Magellan had stopped here as well as most ships making the journey around the Cape of Good Hope. The Azores were just the sort of exotic islands that young men dreamed of. Unfortunately, they did not get a chance to see much of Terceira as they were there just long enough to get a good night's sleep, re-fuel and load anything that might be needed at their next destination.

The base was extremely crowded as it was a critical stop for planes flying from the United States to Southern Europe, Africa and the Far East. There were aircraft coming in or taking off at all hours on their way to and from the different battle fronts. When it came time to leave they sat on the tarmac for hours, waiting their turn behind 30 to 40 other planes. After what seemed like an interminable wait, they finally took off and headed for their next stop in Morocco.

Marrakech is located in the central part of Morocco at the base of the Atlas Mountains. In 1944, Morocco was a French Protectorate and so far, unlike some of its neighbors, it had been spared the ravages of war.

"It reminded me of California. The base commanders considered it dangerous so we never got a chance to get off base to go into the city to see all the great sounding exotic stuff we had heard about from other flyers we'd met in Terceira."

The base was a former French airfield and they stayed in an old hotel taken over by the Air Force. One of the crew was totally perplexed by a certain plumbing fixture that was common in France but uncommon in America. He thought it was for feet washing until he was clued as to its use by Smitty who had been to Europe while in high school.

The next day they flew on to Tunis in Tunisia where they picked up fuel.

"Before the war, Tunisia had been a French protectorate and had a large number of European colonists living there. Although the fighting had been over for more than a year, the city was heavily damaged. Tunisia had been the sight of some of the biggest battles of the North Africa campaign. There were blown up buildings everywhere."

Tunis was the last stronghold of the Germans in North Africa after having been pushed there by the British after the battle of El Alamein. The Americans and Canadians pushed from the west after they regrouped from the pounding they took at the battle at Kasserine Pass. The Nazis were defeated and on May 12, 1943, the Germans and Italians surrendered and the fighting in North Africa ended. Tunis became the staging ground for the Allied push into Sicily and Italy.

The Bobcat's next destination was Cairo in Egypt. As they flew across the Libyan dessert, the crew could see thousands of tracks in the sand and burned out armor from earlier battles spread out below them. Seeing it from the air brought home the sheer magnitude of these battles. As they circled the Pyramids and the Sphinx at low altitude coming in, the whole city was covered in a thick haze from all of the cooking fires. They landed at Payne Field outside of Cairo.

Cairo from the Air

Cairo was under British control during the war. The Nazi Army had tried to take the city three times but was repulsed each time by the British and Indian armies. The great battle of El Alamein was the turning point of the North African War, with the British Army commanded by Field Marshal Bernard Law Montgomery defeating the German Army under Field Marshal Erwin Rommel.

While they were in Cairo, Frank and some of the other crew members hired camels and rode out to the pyramids. Afterwards, they walked about the Old City. They had lunch at the Shepard Hotel and hired a Hansom cab to see more of Cairo. They went to the souk or marketplace and Frank said that if he had been on his way home instead of heading to war, he might have bought some souvenirs. He remembered it was really hot and people were selling orange juice from little stalls and cafés. He and his buddies let the cab go and sat there drinking orange juice while watching the people of Cairo going about their everyday business. It was a brief respite from the war and what lay ahead.

Cairo street scene

"At Payne Field we met a crew returning from the 14th Air Force in China. They told us everything was in short supply there and advised us to load up on all the canned fruit juice we could. "

Frank went to the PX at the field and bought all of the cases he could from the French speaking sales girl. He was somewhat fluent in French as his mother was a Walloon (French speaking) Belgian. He remembered that one of the girls said "he has cute hair" and when he smiled at her, both saw that he knew what she had said. He left Cairo with that warm feeling a young man gets when a pretty girl gives him a smile.

From Cairo they flew to Abbadan in Iran. It was a dry and dusty oil town located on an island in southwestern Iran in the Shat Al Arab waterway. There wasn't much to remember about it except that it was extremely hot and there were a lot of Russian planes there. It was a center for American aircraft being ferried to Russia under the "Lend Lease" program. The base was out in the desert, so he and his crew just waited around for their turn to re-fuel before taking off and climbing above all of the heat and dust.

"From Abbadan, we flew to Karachi in India. We had to wait several days there for our assignment to China. The Air Force had an officers club in an old mansion in the city where the food was good and they had a barbershop and other such

amenities. One night we were walking outside of the club when an Indian driving a hansom cab came along and asked us if we wanted to go to the Gymkhana. We didn't know what it was but it sounded interesting, so we hired him and went."

They were surprised when the cab pulled up in front of the exclusive British officers' club in Karachi. Frank said that the British were polite and hospitable, asking them in for drinks and dinner. When they left, the feelings of goodwill and brotherhood shared that night gave them confidence that they were fighting this Great War together and that America and Britain had each other's back.

Karachi

Their next stop was Agra in India, the home of the Taj Mahal. This was not a scheduled stop, but they wanted to see the great building. They radioed Agra and said that they were having a problem with their gauges and were told to land so they could be checked. As soon as they got on the ground, they hopped in a taxi and drove out to see the incredible building. The reflecting pools that stretch out before it were empty when they got there, but seeing the amazing architecture and hearing its history made the lie they told the tower worthwhile.

The Taj Mahal

Their next destination was Chabua, a city on the Brahmaputra River in Assam State, India. Chabua Airfield was a forward supply base for General Chennault's 14th Air Force in China. From Agra, they flew across India with the Himalayas running parallel to their north. Chabua was located very close to the start of the Burma Road that began at Ledo, crossed into Burma, and ran all the way to China. It was the rear base for the 14th Air Force and had started out as a staging ground for supplies for the Chinese Nationalist Army and for the fledgling "Flying Tiger" squadron based in southern China. In 1941, the Burma Road had become the only land route into China for re-supplying the Nationalist Army. From Lashio in northern Burma, it was 715 miles by truck to Kunming, China. Over this precarious route, only a trickle of supplies arrived at Kunming.

The road was carved out of the steep mountainsides as it snaked its way across Burma and into China. The monsoon rains washed it out regularly and the Japanese bombed and strafed work crews while they tried to make repairs. Breakdowns were the norm rather than the exception as the route went from sea level to up over 14,000 feet and then back down again, making short work of trucks and equipment. The heat, cold, steaming jungles and freezing mountain air sickened men and Malaria was always a problem.

Although very little was ever made public, the Burma Road and
the airlift that followed are some of the most incredible feats
accomplished by the Allies during WWII. At the start of 1942, the
United States was at war with Japan and had begun its effort to
supply the Chinese Nationalist Army with the materials it needed
to fight. The 14th Air Force was flying supplies into a number of
western Chinese airbases as fast as it could. The Japanese already
controlled most of northeastern China and all major Asian coastal
seaports including the British Crown Colony at Hong Kong.

By the spring of 1942, the Japanese controlled French Indochina,
Siam, the Philippines, Singapore, Indonesia, Borneo, New Guinea
and the Solomon Islands. The only countries south of China not in

Japanese hands were Australia and New Zealand. On May 20th
1942, Japanese units completed their capture of Burma (on India's
northern border), cutting off the last significant overland route that
supplied the struggling armies of Generalissimo Chiang Kai-Shek
in China. The United States decided that it had to start a massive
airlift operation that would carry supplies from India, over the
Himalayan Mountains and into China to keep the Nationalist
Chinese going. In April of 1942, American pilots began flying over
the "Hump", as the route was named. All supplies, including gas
earmarked for USAAF squadrons in China, had to travel over the
mountains by air. Over this perilous route, U.S. and Chinese flyers
ferried over 3,500 tons per month to Kunming, the initial
distribution point in China. Many of these missions were flown
with one of the Army/Air Force workhorses, the C-46. It was a
small, two engine aircraft with a surprisingly large lift capacity and
could takeoff and land on a relatively short airfield. Other aircraft
used were the C-47, and the C-87, which was a specially converted
B-24, stripped down to give it more room for cargo.

The dangerous 530-mile long passage over the Himalayan
Mountains took a heavy toll. Nearly 1,000 airmen and over 600
Air Transport Command (ATC) planes were lost over the Hump by
the end of the War.

C-46 Workhorse

The danger came not only from enemy fighters and anti-aircraft fire, but also from the treacherous conditions they faced flying their heavily loaded airplanes over the high mountain passes. The extreme weather could close in so fast many pilots became disoriented. With their limited instrumentation, 125 to 200 mph winds and the violent turbulence buffeting the aircraft, it was not hard to lose a sense of direction, stray away from the route and crash into the sides of the mountains. There were so many aircraft lost along this route that some called it the "Aluminum Trail"; the wreckage of planes could be seen dotting the landscape below.

A large portion of these supplies were flown out of Chabua, located on the Indian side of the Hump. They included everything needed by air and ground operations throughout southeastern China, including fuel. This huge logistical mission was given to the Air Transport Command. The men of the ATC flew supply missions over the Hump, day and night to get the supplies and fuel in.

C-87 Flying over the Hump

It was a huge job and took a tremendous effort to supply the Nationalist Chinese and the 14th Air Force on the China side of the Hump. Said General Harry H. Arnold after arriving in Kunming after the Casablanca Conference:

"A C-87 Liberator transport must consume three and a half tons of 100-octane gasoline flying the Hump over the Himalaya Mountains, between India and Kunming (to get) four tons through to the Fourteenth Air Force. Before a bombardment group can go

on a single mission in its B-24 Liberators, it must fly the Hump four times to build up its supplies".

American and Chinese pilots often flew daily round-trip flights around the clock. Some exhausted crews flew as many as three roundtrips every day. Mechanics serviced planes in the open, using tarps to cover the engines during the frequent downpours, and suffered burns to exposed flesh from sun-heated bare metal. There were not enough mechanics or spare parts to go around and maintenance and engine overhauls were often deferred. Many overloaded planes crashed on takeoff after losing an engine or otherwise encountering mechanical trouble. One pilot recalled flying into Chabua and witnessing four separate air crashes in one day: two C-47s and two C-87s. Due to the lower priority of the CBI theater, parts and supplies to keep planes flying were in short supply and flight crews were often sent into the Himalayan foothills to cannibalize aircraft parts from the numerous crash sites. At times, monthly aircraft losses totaled 50% of all aircraft then in service along the route. A byproduct of the numerous air crashes was a local boom in native wares made from aluminum crash debris.

In his book *Over the Hump*, General William H. Tunner described the significance of the Hump Airlift:

"Once the airlift got underway, every drop of fuel, every weapon, and every round of ammunition and 100 percent of such diverse supplies as carbon paper and C rations, every such item used by American forces in China, was flown in by airlift. Never in the history of transportation had any community been supplied such a large proportion of its needs by air, even in the heart of civilization over friendly terrain...After the Hump, those of us who had developed an expertise in air transportation knew that we could fly anything anywhere anytime."

After a few days of waiting in Chabua, Frank and his men were met by a crew flying in from Kunming who would guide them back across the Hump. Because the route was so hazardous, a green crew like his turned their aircraft over to an experienced crew whose job it was to act as guides and do the flying. They loaded their plane with as much as it could carry without stripping out any armor. Every plane flying out of Chabua west to east was loaded to its maximum weight limit.

Airfield at Chabua

Leaving Chabua, which was located at the head of a long, narrow valley, required that they spiral up, around and around, to gain the altitude they needed to cross the wall of the Himalayas. The floor of the Brahmaputra River valley is only 90 feet above sea level at Chabua. From this altitude, the mountain wall surrounding the valley rises quickly to 12,000 plus feet.

As they climbed, Frank described seeing all of northern Burma, which was dark green jungle except for a big red spot of bare earth where the battle of Myitkyina had been fought. It had been so fierce that the jungle for miles around the air field was completely stripped away, leaving just a huge gaping hole of scorched earth.

Flying eastward out of the valley they had to cross a series of 12,000 to 16,000 foot high ridges, separated by river valleys. The Himalaya Mountains are the source of three of the great rivers of southeast Asia, the Irrawaddy, Salween, and Mekong Rivers and all bisected the route. The "Hump", which gave its name to the whole huge mountainous mass, was the Santsung Range, between the Salween and Mekong Rivers. Frank described looking out the window in wonder as they flew through a valley pass at 12,000 feet, the valley walls towering above them on either side. If anything went wrong up there, their chances were few. If they were lucky enough to successfully crash land, there was no one close enough to mount a rescue effort.

Over the Hump

Chapter Five –Luliang Bridge Club

"Now this is not the end, it is not even the beginning of the end. But it is, perhaps, the end of the beginning." *Winston Churchill*

At dusk, they landed at their new home base in Luliang in Yunnan Province, China.

"We were met by the squadron commander, Colonel Crockett. The first thing he said was 'Who's Padgett?'

I stepped forward and saluted.

'You went to Harvard so you must play bridge.'

Yes sir. I said .

'Report to my tent at 1900 hours.' He said.

"It turned out that Colonel Crockett, the squadron navigator and the squadron bombardier had lost their fourth for bridge and were anticipating my arrival. We played 5 cents a point but I didn't lose a lot."

From that day on, he would play bridge with the Colonel and his friends every Wednesday night.

Control Tower - Luliang

When the Bobcat crew first arrived, the officers "barracks" were still under construction. Frank and the other officers were temporarily quartered in large tents with no running water or heat for the first month. There were mud brick barracks, but the enlisted men got those while the officers waited. All drinking water had to be boiled or disinfected with Halazone tablets before use.

China, 1944

Luliang was situated in the "Valley of Eternal Spring" and the weather lived up to the name. It was cool but not cold in October when they landed and it never got much colder while they were there. The actual field elevation was 5,000 feet and the presence of an 11,000-foot mountain off the end of the runway necessitated executing a hard right turn as soon as they were airborne. This was no easy task when taking off with a full load of bombs and fully topped off fuel tanks. There was a lake in the valley, but like most of the lakes in the area, it was polluted. Frank said it was common that lakes would be full of all kinds of stuff in that part of China. It was not a rice-growing region, but they did farm millet and wheat and there were abundant small family farms growing vegetables.

The airstrip at Luliang had been built by Chinese laborers, who manually crushed the rocks and carried them in woven baskets on top of their heads, or in baskets slung on poles carried over their shoulders. The labor force of men, women, and children, carried out grueling tasks almost entirely by hand. Ox carts delivered rocks; a host of workers with crude picks reduced them to usable stone chips; hundreds more scooped them barehanded into baskets of woven vines, then hand-carried their burdens to the landing strip under construction. The stones were compacted by primitive boulder-filled rollers pulled along by gangs of straining laborers. News photographers recorded the throngs of workers who swarmed back and forth to complete one of many airfields built during the war, a six thousand foot runway near the Yangtze River in China.

Chinese Workers Building Airfield

The airfield was originally built for a squadron of P-40 pursuit aircraft, flown by the Chinese Air Force and members of the American Volunteer Group or AVG. The group was given the popular name, "Flying Tigers" and their shark-faced fighters with flashing teeth and glaring eyes became a much-copied motif painted on the noses of many planes during the war. Later, the group was absorbed into the Fourteenth Air Force under the command of General Claire Chennault. Often forgotten was the 14th's small force of bombers. The 308th Heavy Bomb Group was made up of mostly B-25s with a single group of larger B-24s.

P-40's and B-24 War Paint

The B-24 "Liberators" came to China in the spring of 1943. General Chennault used his small group of "heavies" to support Chinese ground forces, bomb strategic harbors and bridges, and attack shipping in the South China Sea.

The attacks on shipping were often multi-plane missions with bombers taking off at timed intervals at night, covering large areas of the South China Sea, searching for enemy convoys. Without accurate weather forecasts, maps, navigational aids, fighter escorts or the mutually supporting firepower of large formation bombing, their losses were heavy. According to one source, 93 B-24s served in China, and 62 were lost in combat or to other causes. In his memoirs, General Chennault said the following about the 308th Bomb Group:

"They took the heaviest combat losses of any Group in China and often broke my heart by burning thousands of gallons of gas only to dump their bombs in rice paddy mud far from the target. However, their bombing of Vinh railroad shops in Indo-China, the Kowloon and Kai Tak docks at Hong Kong, and the shipping off Saigon were superb jobs unmatched anywhere. When the Army Air Force Headquarters in Washington tallied the bombing accuracy of every bomb group in combat, I was astonished to find that the 308th led them all." General Claire Chennault

The 308th earned its second Distinguished Unit Citation (DUC) for interdiction of Japanese shipping through 1944 and 1945.

Life at Luliang

Life around Luliang was mostly just work for the bomber crews. It wasn't like being stationed in England or other parts of Europe. The airbase was located several miles from the city. Getting to town was difficult since walking was forbidden and rides were scarce. The city was near the front lines and sheltered a huge population of refugees who had fled west, away from the Japanese onslaught in eastern China.

City Gate

There wasn't much fraternizing with the civilian population since very few Chinese spoke English. The food served on base was an attempt at standard American fare. The local farmers raised beautiful vegetables, but because of the nature of the fertilizer they used, fresh produce had to be boiled before serving. The meat was either freshly slaughtered water buffalo or hogs, as the Chinese did not raise cattle. Luliang was located far from any other U.S. base and everything had to be flown in. Food choices were limited. If they had an opportunity, some airmen would go off base to eat at the Chinese restaurants located in town to get a little variety in their diet. The food served in the restaurants was not what these American boys were used to, but sometimes it beat the bland food served in the mess hall. Frank developed a taste for Chinese food so this was not too much of a hardship for him.

Shops in Town

On base, they couldn't leave anything lying around because it would inevitably get "borrowed" by one of the other crews or by the Chinese laborers. When Frank and his crew first arrived, their tent didn't have a stove because someone had taken it, so they went out and walked around base until they found what looked like an empty tent and "borrowed" the stove from it.

Every crew was assigned a Chinese worker called a coolie who did most of the manual labor around the tent, such as sweeping, keeping the coal fired stove stoked and just generally taking care of their needs. This was the way things were done in Luliang and Frank and his crew were "green", inexperienced young guys who did what everyone else was doing. The Chinese laborers were happy because the money they made at the base kept their families alive, and the Americans were freed from housekeeping chores, allowing them to rest between their grueling bombing missions.

Luliang

"By this time, we had moved into our barracks. The buildings were made of mud brick with sheet metal roofs. Each crew had a large room for its four officers with four beds, a table, four chairs, a stove in the middle and a shower in the corner. Water for the shower was supplied by a tank on the roof which was filled by coolies carrying water in buckets from a reservoir tank in the ground."

"Most nights" Frank said, **"At around 10 or 11, a lone Japanese plane would fly into our vicinity, setting off the air raid alarms around the base. When this happened, we would dive into the slit trenches for an hour or so and wait. Someone would always go to the radio shack and play records over the PA system until the all clear sounded. It was called the "Jing Bao Request Program" (jing bao meaning alarm in Mandarin). The Jap plane would drop a bomb somewhere out beyond the field and fly on to the tunes of Glenn Miller or Benny Goodman. Sometimes, it was quite pleasant."**

At night, between missions, there wasn't much to do. Pumped with adrenaline after every mission, flyers found it very hard to come back down again. The men spent much of their free time reading, playing poker or shooting the breeze with their buddies, but even that got boring after awhile. Booze was the choice of many pilots and crews for winding down after returning from a night mission.

If they were lucky, someone they knew might be the 'Officer of the Day', a job that came with the use of jeep. If they had time off they could catch a ride into town and go to one of the restaurants that catered to Americans or, if they had the dough, they could go to one of the bars around town that were in business to sell a little more than just alcohol. These "bars" did a pretty brisk trade in this town at the end of the supply line.

By 1944, the Americans were moving, island by island through the Pacific. British forces had stopped the Japanese thrust into the Plain of Imphal in India, ending their westward drive. The British, along with American and Chinese forces moving down from the north, began to push the Japanese back in Burma.

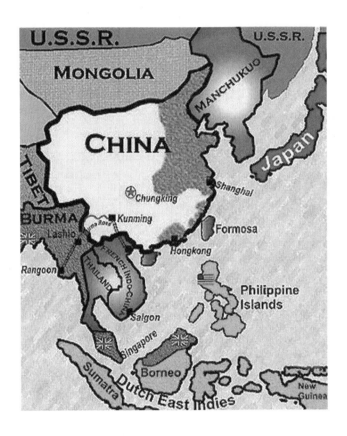

The Japanese were still advancing in eastern China, but the LAB bombing effort by the 14th Air Force was taking a serious toll. From Luliang, the 373rd squadron's primary mission was to patrol and attack Japanese shipping lanes between Burma, China and Pacific islands. While destroying all shipping was their primary objective, they also did land-based bombing over Japanese shipyards in cities like Hangchow, Hong Kong and Canton.

A typical LAB mission involved searching for enemy ships and convoys and attacking them. These missions were always flown at night. A bomb run would often require pilots to fly just above the waves, drop their bombs and then continue on course, hoping that they scored a direct hit so the Japanese gunners couldn't track them. If there were warships among the convoy, they would throw up an incredible amount of antiaircraft fire. These were some of the most dangerous missions of the war, and casualties were high. Many were hit while directly over their target.

If they couldn't find any shipping, it was standard operating procedure to get rid of their bombs on a Japanese air field on Hainan Island or the White Cloud Field at Canton before they landed back at base.

Bombs Away

It was a given to never land with a full bomb load unless there was
no other choice. The B-24 was an unwieldy aircraft and at low
speeds with such a full load, it could be extremely dangerous.
Every pilot knew that landing with a full bomb load was to be
avoided at all costs. If possible, you were to jettison your bombs
where it was safe to do so, preferably, over water.

Almost all missions flown by Frank and the 373rd Squadron were
flown over Japanese occupied territory. Because of this, the crews
were briefed about what to expect if they were shot down or bailed
out behind Japanese lines.

Japan had never ratified the Geneva Prisoner of War Convention of 1929, thus the door was kept open to treating allied prisoners any way they wished. The Japanese high command felt that this was a way to discourage the allies from sending bombing missions over Japanese territories. They felt that allied aircrews would be too intimidated to risk capture by the Japanese.

The Japanese dreaded allied air raids over the overcrowded and poorly built cities of their home islands. Their fears were realized on April 18, 1942 when Tokyo was bombed by a squadron of B-25 bombers launched from aircraft carriers off the coast of Japan. The raid, led by Colonel Jimmy Doolittle, stunned the Japanese high command and its people. Up to this point in the war, they thought their homeland was invincible, now they knew they were vulnerable. Just four months earlier, Japans attack on Pearl Harbor and their seemingly unstoppable onslaught in the Pacific had America reeling. But now, a chink had been found in Japans armor and this knowledge gave a much needed boost to American morale.

Unfortunately, two of Colonel Doolittle's aircraft were captured by Japanese forces in China. The crewmen were interrogated by the Kempeitai and tortured. On 19 October 1942, the Japanese announced that they had tried the crewmen and sentenced them to death, but that several of them had received commutation of their sentences to life imprisonment. No names or details were included in the broadcast.

The story of the Doolittle Raid was splashed all over newspapers in America and was an enormous morale booster for the country. However, the subsequent news of the capture and torture of the crewmen gave notice to allied airmen that they could meet a similar fate if shot down and captured by the Japanese. Frank recalled it was common knowledge at Luliang, that if they were shot down and captured, they would probably be tortured and executed.

Frank's group began flying low altitude radar missions over the Gulf of Tonkin every third night. They flew southeast at around 11,000 feet until they cleared the mountains and were out over the gulf. If they spotted enemy shipping with their radar, they would descend to under 1,000 feet and begin their run in.

Before leaving base, they usually would have an intelligence briefing about the enemy convoys they would be attacking. Sometimes they would just go out hunting, making large sweeps of the Gulf of Tonkin and the South China Sea. Frank told about one time they were out for 13 ½ hours and were so far south that they could see the coast of Luzon in the Philippines on their radar scope. When they got back to Luliang, an American transport gunning its engines at the end of the runway was throwing up a great cloud of dust and messing up the visibility. They had to abort the landing and come around for a second try. As soon as they landed, the two right engines cut out while completing the landing roll. They were completely out of gas.

The morning after this incident, they were awakened at dawn and briefed for a mission against the docks at Hankow.

"The group put up twenty four B-24s, six from each squadron. We flew in our squadron's first echelon of three on the Colonels left wing. We took off about four in the afternoon and assembled over Kunming. When we arrived at the target, it was dark and the city was burning from earlier attacks by B-29s at high altitude and B-25s at low."

"The group bombardier missed the initial turning point, so we were off target on the initial run. Colonel Crockett decided to take our squadron around for a second run. Our target was the dock area where the Han River joined the Yangtze River. Just after the second run, the searchlights caught our plane, which was silver and lit us up so bright that you could have read a newspaper in the cockpit. You could smell the cordite from the exploding ack-ack. The Colonel called me and told me to break formation but I said, 'Colonel, I came with you and I'm leaving with you' and I tightened the interval with his plane. We took no hits from the ack-ack and got back to base

about two in the morning, having just flown 24 hours of combat in a 36 hour period of time."

A couple of days later, Frank and the other officers in his crew hiked out to the nearby mountains and cut down a small pine for their Christmas tree. They decorated it with whatever they could find around the base and set it in a corner of their quarters. This attempt to bring Christmas to their base in southern China was a little sad but it was better than nothing. They were homesick, lonely for their families and America. It was hard for them to muster much Christmas spirit but they did the best they could under the circumstances.

Their luck changed, when right before Christmas, Frank and the crew had to fly their plane to Chabua for an engine change. Chabua wasn't home, but it did have comfortable beds, good food and booze. A black USO troupe was performing when they arrived and they got to see the show. A large number of black truck drivers were also there. The drivers' mission was hauling supplies into Burma. Frank said that one of the entertainers, who he thought was Pearl Bailey, sang "*If I could be with you one hour tonight*", to which one of the truck drivers yelled "*Babe, if only you could*". She responded, "*Suffer you dog, suffer!*" and the whole crowd went crazy, whistling and clapping. Later, Frank went to Midnight Mass in a field chapel with white-washed burlap bags for walls.

Before heading back to Luliang, they went to the PX and stocked up on anything that was hard to get like booze, canned fruit and juices.

"The PX in Luliang was only open on the first Saturday of the month for two hours. You could get Chinese gin, toothpaste and four cartons of cigarettes. We bought them for $1.50 each. We sold them to the Number One boy for $8.00 apiece American money and used that money to buy dinner at the Chinese restaurants outside of the gate or the Chinese Inn in Luliang".

Once a month, one of the flyers was named Officer of the Day. The duty entailed censoring all of the personal outgoing mail, blacking out anything that might give something away to the enemy. The lucky Officer of the Day got a Jeep to go into town. He and the other officers in his crew would go into Luliang to sightsee, shop and eat dinner. The Officer of the Day did have an official reason for going into town, though. It was his responsibility to inspect the brothel nearest the base. Frank claims he never patronized the establishment himself. Apparently this house started when the Japanese overran the base at Guilin. The girls had escaped with the base flight surgeon in an ambulance loaded with all of the infirmary's medicinal alcohol. They had set up shop in Luliang and one of the Officer of the Day's duties was to consult with the flight surgeon as to the "health" of the ladies.

Fueling at Luliang

Life for the airmen at Luliang moved to the beat of the war. Sleep
was not high on the list of things that were considered important by
the command. During the day, the non-stop bombing and fighter
escort missions, added to the constant supply missions, made it
impossible for men to rest. This was also true during the nights.
Nighttime missions flown by the LAB crews and the ceaseless
supply runs, kept the traffic going during the wee hours.
Maintenance crews working around the clock, trying to keep all of
the aircraft operational also added to the din. This made it
extremely hard on the men, but they endured and made do, as did
so many young men like them around the world during this war.

Chapter Six – The 13th Mission

"The eyes of the world are upon you. The hopes and prayers of liberty-loving people everywhere march with you." *Dwight Eisenhower*

B-24 pilots and crews were supposed to fly 400 combat hours before rotating back to the states. Frank and his crew were up to 120 hours on the last day of 1944. In his logbook Frank noted "Mission tonight. Maybe we'll get lucky".

Early on the evening of December 31, 1944, Frank and his crew were briefed on their next mission. A Japanese convoy had been spotted in the Gulf of Tonkin, south of Hainan Island. They were to be the third of four LAB bombers attacking the convoy, leaving Luliang at half hour intervals. The mission was to hit any shipping they could find in order to scatter the vessels so American submarines shadowing the convoy, could pick them off. This was their 13th mission.

"We took off just before dark at 1730 hours. As soon as we got to 11,500 feet, which was the altitude required for getting over the mountains between us and the coast, the bombardier checked the bomb release system. My panel lights did not come on but the bombardier, Harry Sherer, said his were okay so there must be a fuse out on mine. There was no way for us to check on this and we could not go back and land with a full load, so we went ahead with the mission."

The run out to the coast was uneventful as the crew passed the hours talking quietly. Mostly they just flew on in the darkness preoccupied with their own thoughts. Any fears or apprehension were put aside for the moment. Their job was to get there, take care of business and get back to base in one piece. For the most part, keeping the mind busy thinking about home, girls, food, anything, was better than the alternative.

Note: Once a target was picked up on radar, the navigator and bombardier began plotting the position and course for the bomb run, entering the information into the LAB unit. When the pilot had the aircraft on the correct course and altitude for the run in, he turned the controls over to the radar/ bombsight system which took over and began to fly the aircraft and would drop the bomb-load over the target. Once the bombs were dropped, the controls were automatically switched back to the pilots.

"When we got out over the sea, we began to pick up a somewhat scattered convoy on radar. We descended to 600 feet and the bombardier asked the navigator to pick out the largest target. He had us turn in from 22 miles out. As we came closer, the target became two ships alongside each other. The radar operator though they were a cruiser and a destroyer. Sherer, the bombardier, said he would put the bombs between them and get them both. As we came in, the convoy was putting up an intense barrage of antiaircraft fire. We weren't hit on our run in".

B-25 sinks Japanese frigate

"The amount of gunfire coming up from the ships was extraordinary. This was the first time we had been in contact with an enemy warship, much less two, and the sheer firepower directed at us was phenomenal. The tracers were coming up at us like streams and the continuous flashes from the anti-aircraft gun muzzles lit up the decks of the ships."

"The Norden bombsight was flying the plane at this point. It was supposed to automatically pull a pin that let the bomb load go. Normally, when a bomb load is dropped on a ship, there is chaos below. There is panic on the ships deck and hence, a diminished rate of anti aircraft fire. Instead, at the moment of release, our bombs hung up in the racks so we didn't get the lift you normally expected after dropping all that weight. We were a slow moving target with no distractions and the gunners below poured it onto us."

"Almost instantaneously, I heard a loud crack and the right outboard engine immediately ran away, shaking the whole plane violently. I should have feathered the prop right away, but instead I tried to cut back on the RPMs. This worked for a moment, but the engine almost immediately ran away again, screaming with flames shooting out of the cowling. Then it failed altogether. I realized then that some part of the hydraulic system had been hit so we shut the engine down completely."

"We jettisoned our bombs manually and then began trying to climb. The windmilling prop caused the plane to shake very badly and because of the vibrations and the shudder, Clark, the navigator, couldn't get a star fix with his octant. Unfortunately, he had not copied down courses and distances during the emergency, so he couldn't figure out our exact position."

"We climbed through the cloud cover to about 6,000 feet and continued flying northeast. I was on the radio with mayday disaster calls but couldn't raise anyone. We struggled up to 11,500 feet but it was obvious that with the strong headwinds, we were going to have a hard time making it back to base. We should have stayed on the deck, down low and under the clouds. This would have gotten us out of the headwinds until we reached the coast, then we could have started climbing, but we didn't do this. We were young and inexperienced and didn't have faith in the three remaining engines. I thought that at any minute the prop on the burning engine would freeze or fly off, or the heat would reach the fuel lines and blow the wing off. Instead, it just continued to windmill, shaking the plane violently, slowing us down and burning more fuel."

They began sending out a continuous stream of maydays but received no answer. When they were hit, they still had several of hours of fuel left, but the remaining three engines were burning fuel faster than they normally would because of the drag created by the burning engine. It was slowing them down and they had no accurate idea how long their fuel would last.

B-24 hit by flak

The windmilling propeller was turning the main shaft at high speed with no oil pressure. The damaged engine was not engaged, so the oil pump was not sending any lubrication to the main shaft. The heat created by this friction was making their situation critical. Without lubrication, the shaft could freeze up, causing so much drag that they could no longer maintain air speed. Worse yet, the prop could snap off of and fly directly at them, cutting right through the fuselage. The pilots knew this had happened to other aircraft and the tension was palpable as they flew on, sparks and flames spurting from the damaged engine.

"Finally, after about three and a half hours, Gottschall, our engineer, came up on the flight deck and told us that the gauges showed only 15 minutes of fuel remaining."

Frank looked over to Smitty, who shook his head in the negative. If they waited until they ran out of fuel completely, the aircraft would become unstable and make bailing out extremely dangerous. They both knew what they had to do. There was no choice in the matter. They had to ditch the aircraft.

"I gave the order to bail out over the intercom, then snapped on my chestpack and unstrapped myself. I sat back down and took the controls while Smitty unstrapped and put on his parachute. I gave him back the controls and went aft to the bomb bay and found all of the crew still there. Some of them didn't want to jump until everyone went together, others just plain didn't want to jump at all. Some of them were sure that the plane could make it back to base, while others seemed like they didn't understand what was happening. Smitty and I knew that the plane was doomed and we had to get out now, so I pulled my pistol and said 'Jump you bastards before the plane quits flying'. Everyone jumped but the Navigator, Clark, who climbed up the bomb bay doors like a cat. He hesitated just a second, then jumped and I immediately stepped off the catwalk into space. I found myself face up, in a flat spin with a loud rushing noise in my ears."

Chapter Seven – Bail Out

"Step out. Abandon the metal womb, the iron grip of air embrace. Falling fast, the wind roars panic, as thoughts of impact shrill. Grab and pull. SNAP, one hundred eighty to zero. Floating now, slow tranquility. *Anonymous*

This chapter relates each crewmember's experience after bailing from the doomed "Bobcat". It has been adapted from a draft history of the American air war over French Indochina during World War II, written by Martin L. Mickelsen of Athens, GA

What was going through the minds of the Bobcat crewmembers as they jumped from their aircraft can only be guessed. It's safe to say, it was probably not the way they imagined the New Year would begin. The following are the accounts of each man as he touched down.

Traveling at roughly 200 miles per hour, The Bobcat was moving over the ground at a rate of approximately 3-1/3 miles per minute. If each man left the aircraft at five second intervals, it meant they would land between one third to one half mile apart. This doesn't take into account the individual's weight, wind drift and length of time each man waited before pulling his ripcord, but it is reasonable to assume that each man landed within a half mile of the next. Although the distance separating the crew members was not great, where they landed critically impacted the outcome of their individual journeys through enemy territory.

Lieutenant Robert Smith - Pilot landed near the Tonkin town of Voi and was picked up by an Indochinese policeman. He was handed over to a second Indochinese who turned him over to a doctor at a clinic nearby, where he was fed and hidden for a day. The following morning he was disguised as a patient, driven in a private ambulance to an army post at Phu Lang Thuong and turned over to the care of a French Army major, who then drove him to the main army headquarters in the Citadelle in Hanoi.

Staff Sergeant Hugh C. Pope - Nose Gunner, a six year veteran of the Army/Air Force, hit the ground in an old Chinese cemetery. On impact, he twisted his ankle on a tombstone. Dazed and a little befuddled, he gathered his parachute and hid in a ditch that ran alongside the cemetery. As he stood on the roadside, a number of Indochinese came by and he asked each for help, but no one could understand him. Finally a boy, who seemed to understand a little English, indicated he should walk along the road to a train station. As he limped along, a truck approached and he waved it down. It turned out to be a French Army truck. The French soldiers stopped and helped Pope climb aboard. They told him that they were friends and they were looking after some of his crewmates.

As **Staff Sergeant William D. Sanderson - Tail Gunner** bailed out of the "Bobcat," he spotted the parachute of another crewman floating down nearby. Sanderson landed in a field, gathered his chute, and hid inside a stand of trees until morning. He began walking along a road and soon a French Army truck came along and stopped for him. As Sanderson jumped up into the back, he was surprised to see Pope sitting there. The French truck carried the sergeants to what they described as an "insane asylum" which had a small infirmary where Pope's leg was bandaged.

Corporal John J. Webster - Ball Turret Gunner was one of the last crewman to jump from the Bobcat. He landed in an irrigation ditch and hid on a nearby hill until the next morning when he attempted to find help. He heard someone nearby whistling "Tipperary," the signal that the French used to identify themselves as friends. The whistler was one of a two-man French civilian underground search party. However, Webster, like all the other crewmembers of the "Bobcat", did not know about this signal as it was never mentioned in any of their briefings. Webster approached the two French civilians anyway and they took him to the "asylum" where he met up with Pope and Sanderson.

Staff Sergeant Joseph P. Medon - Radar Operator from Wilkesbury Pennsylvania, had landed near the railroad tracks a couple of miles southeast of the clinic. He was found by a group of friendly Indochinese and taken to their village. An Indochinese from the clinic came to the village, gave him some civilian clothes, and took him to the "asylum" where he joined the others.

Sergeant George Uhrine - Top Turret Gunner, from Dearborne Heights Michigan, landed hard when a gust of wind slammed him into the ground of a cemetery. It was a different cemetery than the one where Pope had landed. He sustained a compound fracture to his leg and was knocked out when his head hit a tombstone. Fortunately, he was found by friendly Indochinese civilians who helped him get to the "asylum" on a bamboo stretcher.

Lieutenant Everett A. Clark - Navigator had landed near a rice paddy and was immediately joined by **Bombardier Lieutenant H. W. Sherer**, who landed near him. The two were found by a French army patrol the next morning. They were given French enlisted men's uniforms and put in the back of a truck with four French soldiers.

Radio Operator Sergeant Stanley J. Brach, and Engineer Sergeant William Gottschall had been sighted moving northwest but they had not been seen since. This information was passed to Lieutenant Smith from French underground sources. No one had seen **Co-Pilot Lieutenant Frank Padgett**.

Chapter Eight - Frank New Year's Day, 1945

"Without belittling the courage with which men have died, we should not forget those acts of courage with which men have lived. The courage of life is often a less dramatic spectacle than the courage of a final moment, but it is no less a magnificent mixture of triumph and tragedy." *John F. Kennedy.*

"I waited until I was almost in the clouds then gave a tentative pull on the ripcord. Nothing happened, so I gave it a good jerk and the chute came loose. It opened and with a snap, jerked me upright. I hadn't fastened the harness tightly and the straps between my legs gave me an uncomfortable jolt. Before jumping I had holstered my pistol so I had the ripcord in my left hand and a flashlight in my right as I fell."

Dropping through the cloud layer at 5,000 feet, it became clear to Frank that he was over land. He could tell this, not from being able to see the features of the land below, but because a dog was barking somewhere off in the distance. What he saw could have just as easily been the surface of the ocean, the twinkling lights below fishing sampans spread out over the broad expanse of the sea. If this were the case, he and the rest of the crew would be in dire straights. They had no life preservers and wore full length flight suit and boots. Even slowed by their parachute, they would have plunged down under the surface when they hit the water. Getting tangled in the shrouds underwater would have been deadly, even for a strong swimmer like Frank.

Instead, thanks to the barking dog, he was sure that he was coming down over dry land. Where, he did not know exactly. He was hoping that they had made it back over China and friendly territory before ditching the plane, but he wasn't sure. He might be over French Indochina, which would not be a good thing because it was held by the Japanese. Frank could still hear their plane as it continued on its now unmanned journey north, the sound of the engines slowly fading away. His thoughts briefly replayed the rushed decision they had made a few minutes before, hoping he had done the right thing when he ordered the crew to bail out. Some of them had not wanted to jump, but he had done what he felt was the right thing. There had been no time to be nice about it. They were in imminent danger and he and Smitty had agreed there was no choice but to ditch the aircraft. If anyone wanted to question his actions, they were welcome to do so when they got back to China. He quickly pulled himself back together and focused on his immediate situation.

The smell of the land rose up to greet him, the rich, cloying smell of rotting vegetation and damp earth. He could now make out some of the features of the land below. He could see what appeared to be cultivated fields, probably rice paddies with tree lines separating them. The scattered lights he saw were coming from little groups of houses and out buildings spread over the flat land.

The dog had stopped barking and all was quiet except for the faintly receding sound of the plane's engines and the quiet "whoosh" of the air as it passed through the shrouds of his parachute. Frank began to prepare himself for the inevitable, jarring impact of landing. He tried to remember what he had been told to do in parachute training. Unfortunately, training had been a short "how to" with no actual jumps or even practice jumps from a tower. He had never thought he would have to actually bail out of his plane and he cursed the lack of training. He hoped that he would touch down in one of the fields, not one of the tree lines, as he had heard of the consequences of landing in the trees. A slight feeling of panic began with thoughts flashing through his mind of crashing through sharp tree branches and the damage this could cause a man. He did not dwell on this and focused on the looming reality of landing.

Watching someone parachuting in a movie, they seemed to be gently floating down. This had been the case moments before while he still had some altitude. Everything had seemed so serene, as if in slow motion. But now, everything accelerated, the ground was approaching fast and he began to tighten his muscles, bracing himself for the inevitable collision. Frank remembered what they told him in training about trying to loosen up and roll with it. He quickly forced himself to relax as the ground came up to meet him, 100 feet, 50 feet, 20 feet. His boots slammed into the earth accompanied by an incredible body jolt.

"I hit the ground in a dry rice paddy. I rolled onto my back, the wind knocked out of me. I lay there shaking off the cobwebs and checking to see if I had broken anything. I sat up cautiously, sure someone must have heard me hitting the ground, but looking around, I saw no one. The dog in the distance began barking again and others joined in. I wondered for a moment if they might be barking at someone from my crew. The wind was calm on the ground, so as soon as I got my breath back, I unstrapped my harness and gathered my chute. Staying low, I ran to a stand of trees. I found an old hollowed out stump and stuffed my parachute into it. I took out my compass and started walking north. Before each mission, they gave us our chutes and a canvas pouched belt containing, they said, maps on silk and Indian Rupees. I walked for awhile, coming to a dirt road with a kilometer stone giving the towns in either direction. I went for the packets containing the silk maps only to find they had been slit open and the maps removed. I had no way of knowing where I was, except that because the writing on the kilometer marker was in the Roman alphabet, I was sure I was somewhere in Tonkin Province, French Indochina. I realized then that I was in great danger and had no idea which way it was to safety."

The maps that were supposed to be in the pouch were of China, French Indochina, Burma and Siam, beautifully printed on silk with a message on the reverse side explaining that America would reward anyone who helped the flyer return to friendly lines. These maps were considered a valuable souvenir and were often removed by ground crewmen who serviced the planes and equipment, to send to friends and family back home. Without a map to guide him, Frank realized that his only chance of making it back to friendly territory was to travel at night in a northwesterly direction, hoping to remain undetected.

Frank moved away from the road, following it at a distance, hoping that he might come across one of his crew. He was exhausted, but kept walking until he found a stand of bamboo where he lay down to rest. He tried his best to stay awake but quickly fell into a deep sleep.

The sun was just beginning to come up when he was awakened by the prodding of a hoe wielded by a man standing over him. The man appeared to be a village peasant, probably a farmer. He was a small man, very thin, wearing loose, black clothing and the conical straw hat commonly worn by peasant farmers in Asia. The man spoke to him but Frank could not understand him. He wished that he had the missing map so he could show it to this man and hopefully get some help. Frank tried to speak to the man in English asking **"Do you speak English?"**. When he got only puzzled looks, he tried French of which he knew a little, **"Parlez-vous Français?"** Unfortunately, the man did not respond to either.

For many years prior to WWII, Indochina had been ruled as a colony by the French. In the cities, many Indochinese had become fluent in French but usually not in the countryside. During WWII, when the Japanese invaded Indochina, they allowed the French Vichy government to continue as administrators because the Vichy French were allies of the Axis. The French regularly turned allied flyers shot down over Indochina over to the Japanese. Captured flyers were interrogated and tortured by the Japanese. Some were executed. Frank and his crew had heard about this and took it as a given that if shot down and captured, they would be executed. It was a threat they carried in the back of their minds whenever they were on missions over French Indochina. Because this was Japanese held territory, Frank knew the likelihood of getting betrayed by the local populace was high, especially since the

Japanese offered rewards to the Indochinese for turning in U.S. flyers. Those (native Indochinese) caught giving aid to enemy flyers were tortured and imprisoned.

"Indochina had been occupied by the Japanese since mid 1941. The French colonial army was there but it was supposedly still loyal to the Vichy French government which had ruled over Vietnam, Laos and Cambodia for many years. I had no intelligence briefings on the situation in French Indochina and I didn't know who to trust. I learned later that by the time I was shot down, the French were supposed to pick up any downed airmen and send them back to China. The French were supposed to patrol the area where many of the American planes were coming down, whistling 'Tipperary' to make contact. None of us knew about this 'Tipperary' business, and even if we heard it, we didn't know what to make of it."

If Frank had known the French were now helping allied flyers, it might have made a difference in what happened to him. If he had been aware of this, he would probably have sought out the French while evading the Indochinese. Without this knowledge, he was at a serious disadvantage as he tried to make his way to safety.

The man with the hoe signaled with his hand to follow and led the way to a small village that Frank could now see through the trees. With no other options, Frank followed for a while but deciding that he was being led into a trap, he took off, running away from the road and into the bushes where he hid again. He took inventory of what little he had. Besides the 45-caliber pistol and compass, he had one clip of ammunition, a knife, and a couple of bars of hard chocolate.

The gravity of the situation really hit home when he realized how dire his predicament was. He was a tall, white Caucasian without food or water, wandering around a densely populated Asian country, inhabited by people who may or may not be friendly. Frank realized that his chances of making it back to allied territory were not great. He wasn't sure about the distance to the Chinese border, nor did he know the best route to get there because of the missing map. He ate some of his chocolate bar and tried to sleep a little. It was New Years Day 1945.

That night he moved north until he found a spot to rest, hidden in a bamboo grove. When he woke in the early afternoon, he was thirsty and hungry. He saw a hamlet across the paddies about a half mile away and decided to head towards it. It was early evening by the time he drew close to the small village. As he approached, he noticed that there was a little stream he had to cross. He went down the bank to get a drink of water. As he began drinking, a villager leading a water buffalo came upon him.

The man gestured for Frank to follow him into the village. Because he was so hungry and tired, he followed. The man led him to a small house where he was given some food by the man's wife. Sitting there, he began to relax a little. The house had a swept dirt floor and walls of bamboo with window openings. The breeze blowing through the cracks in the walls and the windows made it pleasantly cool inside. The roof was thatched and the rafters were hung with tools and farm implements, as well as baskets of what he did not know. There was a sleeping platform and a low, rough-hewn table. It was obvious that the owner was a man of few means, and the chicken Frank was eating was not their every day fare. As he was eating, other villagers began to collect around the house to see the American flyer. All seemed peaceful and calm, so he relaxed a little. He sat on a mat in a corner and soon fell asleep.

Chapter Nine - Betrayed

Courage is the first of human qualities because it is the quality that guarantees all the others.
Winston Churchill

Frank woke up to the sounds of truck doors slamming and guttural commands shouted and knew that he had been betrayed to the Japanese. Grabbing his shoes, he jumped out of the window and started running. He smashed his foot on a rock and went down. As he rolled over and began to rise, he was surrounded by several Japanese soldiers. They were angry and shouting, gesturing with their rifles for him to get back down on the ground. They kicked him and hit him until he submitted; they bound his wrists and ankles and put him into the back of the truck. He was the only prisoner in the truck. There were a couple of Japanese soldiers as well as an Indian National Army (INA) soldier to guard him. The Indian soldier was a member of the INA, which was the military wing of the Provisional Government of Free India.

The INA was allied with the Japanese and the Indian soldier was hostile and unfriendly. Although he spoke English, he gave Frank no help. Any questions Frank asked were answered with angry glares and terse monosyllables. The Japanese soldiers would jab him with their rifles whenever he tried to talk. They drove for about twenty minutes before stopping at what seemed to be a Japanese police rural jail. They did not interrogate him there, only asking basic questions which he did not answer. They gave him a little water and rice but nothing else.

The weather in northern Indochina was quite chilly at this time of year and he slept on the jail's hard cement floor with no blanket or mat to separate him from the cold concrete. After two days, he was put in a truck and driven to the main Kempeitai jail in Hanoi. This time he was handcuffed and shackled. It took about an hour before the truck pulled up to an old nondescript, two-story building where he was hustled out and down into the basement. There was a sign above the entryway as he passed through that said "Defense de fumer" which meant no smoking in French. He concluded that this had been some sort of French colonial administration building before the Japanese took over.

While Frank was entering the Hanoi Kempeitai jail, his crewmates Clark and Sherer were already crossing back into China. Picked up shortly after landing by the French patrol, they were taken to the French fort at Lang Son near the border. At Lang Son, they were given Sten guns by the French officer in charge and he walked with them towards the border. A mile inside the frontier, the American fliers were turned over to Chinese soldiers who were waiting for them. The Chinese took them to the Chinese village of Luong Ban on the 3rd of January.

Frank was exhausted and hurting from the beating he had been given when captured, feeling dazed as he stumbled down the long hallway. The guards were jerking him around and pushing him and he fell. They immediately dragged him to his feet and pushed him on down the hall.

Kempeitai with samurai swords

The building he had just entered was a jail run by the Kempeitai, the Japanese equivalent of the Nazi Gestapo. The Kempeitai were guilty of some of the worst atrocities of World War II. They were not front line soldiers and were not intended to fight in any battles. Instead they dealt with civilians and POW's who had no way of fighting back. They were responsible for rear areas in battle zones, running POW camps and for reprisal raids against civilian populations. In some Japanese occupied countries, they singled out entire districts and deliberately put them to the torch. Men, women, and children were ruthlessly slaughtered.

Kempeitai officers

The Kempeitai were indoctrinated with a twisted version of Bushido, the ancient Japanese military code, calling for a soldier to die rather than suffer the shame of surrender. In their eyes, Allied prisoners of war were thought to have lost all honor by surrendering and were treated with great cruelty. The Kempeitai often executed captured allied pilots and Frank knew that his chances of living through this day were awfully small. He was thrown in a large cell and interrogated. They asked where he was based, who his superiors were, what type of aircraft had he flown and were there others like him. Up to this point, Frank felt that the interrogators didn't know whether he was a bomber pilot with a crew, or a fighter pilot by himself so he didn't answer their questions.

"You were only supposed to give your name, rank and serial number, but after they beat you and burn you enough, it gets harder and harder to keep silent."

Then began a routine that changed only when an interrogator decided to use his imagination and try something new.

The pen and ink illustrations are taken from the book, "La Kempetai", illustrated by French prisoners of the Kempetai after the war. They depict the brutal realities that awaited those who entered the Kempetai jails.

DEPART POUR L'INTERROGATOIRE, Copyright 1947 G.H.P.

"I think they broke my nose and they burned me on the cheek, neck and back with a lighted cigar, pushing it in until it went out. I could smell my flesh burning and hear it sizzle whenever they did this. They demanded I give them the name of our group commander or they would execute me. I told them to go ahead."

One day they forced him to kneel down with one of them standing over him with a samurai sword, and they told him they were going to chop his head off.

"Finally, they made me kneel down and put a Samurai sword to the back of my neck. They again demanded I give them our

commander's name or they would execute me. I told them to go ahead."

When he didn't cry or beg for his life, they laughed at him and then proceeded to kick and punch him down. This went on for days until Frank was unable to get up when they came for him. He lost track of time, only knowing the difference between day and night. He began to slowly and grudgingly give up information, but it was basically useless because he truly didn't know much. His hope was that they would finally figure out that he didn't have any valuable information and stop hurting him.

After five days in solitary with beatings every day, no sleep and only enough water to keep him alive, they loaded him into a car and drove across Hanoi to another nondescript building and hustled him inside. This was the Headquarters of the Kempeitai and it sent fear down his spine. Frank was handcuffed with his elbows behind his back and his ankles shackled. He was led up a flight of stairs, then down a hallway and stopped before a door. He could hear someone screaming somewhere in the building. It was a terrifying shriek of agony and despair and it shook him to the core. One of the guards knocked on the door, opened it and pushed Frank through. A quick glance revealed an office with a small library of books standing against the back wall. A large wooden desk sat in front of the bookshelves with several chairs gathered in front of it. Some picture frames with what seemed to be diplomas hung on the other walls.

"There was a middle aged Japanese man in a leather jacket sitting behind a desk. He had them take off the handcuffs and asked me to sit down after dismissing the guards. He asked me if I would like a cup of tea and I said yes."

The man looked to be in his late thirties or early forties. He was of average height and build and had a moustache and black hair, neatly combed back from his forehead. Speaking in slightly accented English, he invited Frank to sit, motioning him to a chair. He said that he was a colonel in the intelligence wing of the Kempeitai, which made Frank extremely uneasy. When the tea came, the colonel began.

"You went to Harvard. I am a graduate of Columbia myself, but I went to summer school at Harvard in 1921". He said how much he admired the United States and the freedoms that the people enjoyed. "Now, what is this nonsense about you not knowing your group commander?"

Frank began to repeat his story about not knowing that information when the Colonel held up his hand to stop.

"The Colonel unrolled a scroll with the complete TO (Table of Organization) of our group on it and pointed to the name in the box marked Group Commander."

"Is that it?" he said.

"It could be but I really don't remember for sure."

"I'll put down that you said yes."

With that, the Colonel completed the form in front of him, stamped it and put it in his desk. He asked Frank how long he thought the war would last. Frank thought the war might go on for another two or more years.

"No, you will be home by Christmas." said the Colonel. "Now, I am going to tell you what is going to happen to you. We have two sergeants from your crew here and we are going to send all of you to Saigon in a week. I will put my chop on your papers so they will not torture or kill you, but there must be no funny business from you. You must do what they tell you and even if they hit you, you must not fight back. While you are here, I'll send for you every couple of days to get you out of your cell and we'll talk about Harvard and America. I'll say it is further interrogation."

Frank now knew that at least two of his sergeants had been captured. He did not know which of the sergeants they were and he wondered if any of their crewmates had managed to escape. For the next few days, he was taken across town to meet with the Colonel to talk about New York, Cambridge and the state of the world. This was not how prisoners were usually treated, but the common ground that these two men found probably saved Frank from the fate of many other captured flyers. This routine of going back and forth from his cell to the Colonel's office went on for a number of days.

"One day, I was led in and there were two men in the Colonel's office who claimed to be university professors and they wanted to talk about American morale at home. Well, it had been awhile since I had been there and so I mainly just listened to them. They told me about the Battle of the Bulge in Europe and that the end of the war was near for Germany. The Russians were steadily advancing from the east, while the allies were rushing in from the west. This was good news and cheered me up considerably. Despite the bleak outlook for their Axis partners in Europe, Japan would definitely fight on they said."

While Frank was undergoing interrogation, Sanderson, Pope and Uhrine were moved to Lanessan Hospital in Hanoi where Pope and Uhrine stayed, being treated for their leg injuries. Sergeant Sanderson was given a French soldier's uniform and taken to the Citadelle in Hanoi where he met up with Lieutenant Smith.

145

Clark and Sherer were moved to Tsingsi in China on the 4th
arriving back in Luliang on January 12th.

Webster and Medon remained at the "asylum" for another day,
then were transferred to the home of a Frenchman named Jean
Counard, a member of General Léopold Giraud's underground
group. The next day they were taken to the home of another
Frenchman, a prominent attorney named Bonat, whose uncle was
General de Gaulle's Minister of Colonies. Several days later, the
two were taken to the French legion camp at Ba Vi where they
were given civilian clothing and Bonat then returned them to
Hanoi. In a bizarre turn, he gave them a tour of the Indochinese
capital in his car, despite the fact that the streets were full of
Japanese. Medon later said, "We were extremely nervous as we
drove past the Japanese army post near the center of the city." As
a treat, Bonat then took them to a movie theater where they
watched the American film, "Dagwood and Blondie", while sitting
surrounded by Japanese soldiers. This was surely one of the more
bizarre episodes of the Pacific war. After the movie, they went
back to Monsieur Bonat's house and remained there for a week
while arrangements were made by the underground to help them
escape back to China. They were dressed as French soldiers and
given fake French identification cards. Although they left for the
Chinese border in a truck, it broke down and they had to walk the
rest of the way. "We were pursued much of the way by the

Japanese who discovered we had escaped" Medon later recalled.

Frank had only the Kempeitai Colonel's word that he, and his two crewmates were now under the Colonel's protection and that it would keep them safe from execution. The Colonel had stamped their papers with his chop and said that it would protect them as they were sent south. Frank had no way of knowing if this was true, but had no choice except to put his faith in it being so. Sometimes, bonds between men are formed for reasons that may not be apparent to others. In this case of fortuitous coincidence, the Colonel's admiration of the freedoms he saw while getting his education in America and the fact that he and Frank had gone to the same school, were enough for him to place Frank and his men under his direct protection.

Chapter Ten - Journey South

The wise man in the storm prays God not for safety from danger, but for deliverance from fear.
Ralph Waldo Emerson

"Finally, I was taken from my cell to the railroad yards in Hanoi. The Japanese brought Gottschall, our engineer, and Brach our radioman and turned us over to a platoon of Japanese infantry being sent by boxcar to Saigon. This was the first time I had seen Gottschall and Brach since bailing out, and even though I wasn't happy to see they had been captured, I was glad to be with them. I didn't feel so alone now."

The train was crowded with soldiers and Frank, Brach and Gottschall were handcuffed and shackled. Slowly, they began the journey south. The narrow gauge tracks ran The train ran a few miles inland from the coast and moved only by night to avoid detection by allied aircraft looking for moving targets. By day they would stop and try to camouflage the train. The going was slow because there were many rivers in Indochina and allied aircraft had already knocked out most of the bridges linking north and south.

Destroyed bridge

If it was a big river, the guards would herd them off the train and onto a ferryboat for the river crossing. They would board another train to continue the journey south. These crossings were the most dangerous of the trip. The land around these bridges had been bombed so often that the ground was totally barren and there was no place to hide. The ferryboats the Japanese pressed into service were small river craft and not very stable when fully loaded. Being shackled while crossing a river could be a death sentence if they capsized and Frank asked them to remove their shackles, but the commander refused.

The soldiers foraged for food in the towns they stopped in each night. Frank said he and his crewmates were given the same food as the Japanese soldiers. He recalled it was decent food because the Japanese cooks were skilled at making palatable meals from whatever was available. Apparently, bad cooks were not tolerated in the Japanese army.

"One day we spent in a Buddhist monastery on a hill where the monks fed us. They were very kind. I could see the compassion in their eyes as they came and placed the food in front of me. By this time I was suffering from Amoebic dysentery and beginning to get weak. The Japanese soldiers seemed to be having the same problem, so they were making frequent relief stops. One day, a French civilian family came to stare at we three American prisoners. I'm not sure what they were feeling, seeing us sitting by the side of the road, shackled together. They were the only Caucasian faces we saw in the ten day journey."

"We were forbidden to talk to each other but we would whisper together when the guards weren't looking. We were all feeling sick because of the dysentery and being shackled together made the train ride a most miserable experience. We were not always able to hang on until the train stopped, and this made everything worse."

At one stop, Frank remembered the soldiers used the townsmen's nets and caught some large fish from the river. The cooks made rice, vegetables and fish. He and the other two airmen were very grateful to get a nourishing meal since all they had eaten for the last six days was some rice and bits of vegetable.

"I was dressed in coveralls and long johns when captured and still had the same clothes on. The coveralls were apparently treated with some kind of insect repellant, but the long johns were not. The three of us had picked up lice in the cells in Hanoi. They were crawling all over me and itched like crazy. The Japanese commander became aware of this and one day we stopped in a town with a park-like area and ponds and they got a big cast iron kettle from the village, filled it with water and built a fire beneath it."

The commander ordered Frank, Gottschall and Brach to strip and wash themselves with the buckets of the hot water. When they finished, he had the guards dump their clothes into the boiling water, killing the lice and cleaning the clothes at the same time. It was a luxury to put on clean clothes, even if they were still damp. This courtesy was one of those instances that made Frank aware of the different treatment they received from Japanese Army regulars versus the Kempeitai. Many of the soldiers on the train were ordinary men whereas the Kempeitai guards seemed to be another breed, hostile and indifferent.

As they traveled south, Frank and his crewmates began to see more destruction from allied bombing. One afternoon they were stopped at a river crossing, waiting for the cover of darkness when an American B-25 came flying up the river towards them. The bridge had been bombed flat except for a small section still standing. Everyone dove for cover in the drainage ditches at the side of the road. The B-25 dropped a couple of bombs on what was left of the bridge. As it passed overhead, a Japanese private stood up and began firing his rifle at it. Someone in the B-25 noticed the muzzle flashes and it immediately banked into a hard turn, dropped down low over the road and began a strafing run with its four 50 cal. machine guns blazing. After two passes, the plane flew off, its crew never knowing who they had been shooting at.

"Getting shot at is an experience I will never forget. There is only so deep a human can burrow into hard packed earth, but I tried as hard as I could to go deeper yet. I am still amazed that no one was hit, because I am sure the Japanese would have executed us on the spot."

When the plane had gone, the commander called for the soldier who had done the shooting. As the man came forward, the commander beat him down, berating him for his stupidity. Doing this would have been unthinkable in an American Army, but corporal punishment was common in the Japanese Army and line soldiers suffered severe beatings quite often for little reason.

B-25 after strafing run

At night when they were waiting to cross a river, the Japanese guards took the prisoners down to the river to wash and relieve themselves. Once, as Frank was crouching down by a river, a hand wrapped around his mouth from behind and a voice with a French accent whispered *"American?"*. Frank nodded quickly and the hand came away. Later, a Japanese guard told him that this happened with some regularity to Japanese troops, except their throats were cut. The guard told him that when trains were bringing wounded Japanese soldiers to Saigon after losing the battle of Moulmein in Burma, the injured were placed on pallets beside the train so they could rest. The French would sneak up and slit their throats. The Japanese and the French despised each other even though they were allies.

While Frank, Brach and Gottschall, were on the train moving south towards Saigon, lieutenant Smith and Sergeant Sanderson were hiding at the French Army Headquarters. They left the Citadelle dressed as French soldiers and were taken by a French captain to Lao Kay on the Sino-Vietnamese border. But because the road was so bad, the captain was forced to turn back. He instead took them to Ha Giang where they were hidden in a deserted blockhouse and given French civilian clothing. At 10 p.m. they left again and were handed off to various French soldiers until they reached Thanh Thuy on January 13th. Then they were taken across the frontier to Pac Bao and turned over to the Chinese. They finally reached their base at Luliang on January 18th, in an L-5 "Sentinel" aircraft.

Now, six of the Bobcat crew were back in China. This left Pope and Uhrine still at Lanessan hospital and Padgett, Brach and Gottschall unaccounted for.

Chapter Eleven - Fight to Survive

"To a prisoner of war, the enemy is everywhere. He controls your fate, your future, even your bodily functions. You are at war at every second. You are never given leave. You can never leave the combat zone." *Unknown*

January 15, 1945

After ten days of travel, the prisoners reached Saigon on January 16, 1945. They were taken to the Kempeitai jail in Cholon, the Chinese section of Saigon. The jail was located in a converted school named Ecole Chee Yung, Ecole meaning school in French. Frank recalled that there was a church somewhere nearby and he could hear the bells every day. Frank, Gottschall and Brach would spend the next five months in the Kempeitai jail.

As they were led into the building, an all consuming dread closed in around Frank. The guards who had brought them from the train turned and left and Frank, Gottschall and Brach were quickly surrounded by their new captors. They had no idea what to expect. One of the Kempetai men who seemed to be in charge took the papers that the train guards had handed over. These looked to Frank like the papers that the colonel in Hanoi had stamped with his chop. Would it carry any weight here? The guard growled "Pajet" and Frank looked up. The man motioned for him to stand and he said something to the other guards. They grabbed Frank under the arms and dragged him down a corridor, lined on both sides with what seemed to be cages with thick timbers instead of bars. He could see that there were people inside of the cages but because there was little light, could not make out who they were.

The stench of human waste overwhelmed him as they reached the far end of the corridor, opened the timber framed door to a cell and pushed Frank in. As the guards slammed and locked the door, Frank looked around his cell, overcome with a feeling of despair. Two weeks ago, he had been a free man fighting the very men who now had absolute control over him, men he knew to be brutal predators who thought nothing of taking the life of a prisoner like himself. He sat down on the rough wooden floor at the far end of the four by eight foot cell. He thought of home, his parents and his life before the war. It seemed so very long ago, almost a dream. Like most men who find themselves in dire circumstances they never could have imagined, Frank began to question his God. Why? What had he done to deserve this? He thought about the colonel in Hanoi and what he had said. Would his chop really protect them?

RECEPTION

Copyright 1947, G.H.P.

From the day they arrived, the three Americans were
systematically starved while being forced to live in the most
deplorable conditions. Frank, already sick with amoebic dysentery,
began his journey down a slippery slope of illness and starvation.
Sometimes the fliers were in solitary confinement, other times
together in the same cell.

Every cell in the prison was reinforced with heavy lumber to
prevent escape. The front wall was made of the same materials but
was built like a cage. There was a door with a slot where the
guards slid the food to the prisoners. The floor was wood, very
rough-sawn, with cracks between the planks. It was extremely hot

and they were told to lie there day and night without moving. Talking or whispering were forbidden and reprisals were severe if they were caught.

LE NOUVEAU

"...Des homes immobiles, accroupis, buste nu, visage émacie, envahi d'une barbe qui accentue leur de détresse font face aux grilles." *Copyright 1947, G.H.P.*

"Most of the prisoners were Japanese soldiers who had committed some kind of offence. When we first arrived, there were three British prisoners. We weren't supposed to talk or stand up, but when the Japanese guards were not around, the Brits told us from their cell across the corridor, that they were there because they had been on a work detail and one of them had told another to 'bugger off'. The Japanese guards had heard this and thought they had said 'bukaro', one of the 'few

Japanese curse words, and thought it had been aimed at them."

It was a very high price to pay for the misinterpretation of a word.

O TIA!

"Arrosée d'une gorge d'eau bouillante dans un bol collectif.", *Copyright 1947, G.H.P.*

"Our diet was a bowl of rice gruel in the morning, a small bowl of rice at noon and another bowl with possibly some cooked vegetables in the evening. Along with this, we got hot water that was called "Ocha", which meant tea in Japanese, but unfortunately it contained no tea. I steadily lost weight and began to suffer from malaria and beriberi. The malaria was from the mosquito bites that covered my body. Beriberi is a

159

vitamin deficiency disease and there are two types, "wet" and
"dry". The wet type causes water to accumulate in your
extremities and it can be fatal. This was the type that I had. I
could press my thumb into my ankle and the depression it left
would be there for hours. I also had amoebic dysentery, which
caused dehydration. The two together were very bad. The
malaria would flare up every two weeks or so and I would lie
there alternating, shivering and sweating for 3 or 4 days until it
would let up."

REVES

"…On couchait sur le sol, éclairs toute la nuit par la lumière électrique.".

Copyright 1947 G.H.P.

"We were given a tatami mat, a blanket and a rice husk pillow.
They took our coveralls and gave us each a loin cloth in return.

160

There was an open bucket in the corner for a toilet, which was emptied once a day. Using the bucket was a miserable and embarrassing experience because I had dysentery and had go so often and there was no water to wash. We slept on the floor on the tatami with the rice husk pillow. The lights were always on at night and the mosquitoes swarmed. I'd put the blanket over me despite the heat and the cockroaches would get under it and I could feel their twitching feelers as they crawled over me."

"About once a month, ants would swarm up through the floor boards and carry away all the roaches, spiders and other insects. We would sit on our mats and watch while the ants did this. They never came onto our mats, they just swarmed up, killed the other insects and carried them away."

The effects of amoebic dysentery, beriberi and malaria were whittling away Frank's natural defenses. The accumulation of water in his feet, ankles and elbows caused excruciating pain. The malaria would come in waves that alternated between raging fevers and bone wracking chills that he could not stop. The dysentery kept his digestive system in a state of gut wrenching pain. He was desperate for nourishment, but there was no way to get food in from the outside.

PATURE

"....Trois fois par jour, une boule de riz de la grosseur d'une orange est jetée aux prisonniers. *Copyright 1947, G.H.P.*

Starvation causes the body to lose fat and muscle mass. The body breaks down these tissues in order to produce energy. Catabolysis is the process of a body breaking down its own muscles and other tissues in order to keep vital the nervous system and heart muscles functioning. Vitamin deficiency is a common result of starvation, often leading to anemia, beriberi, pellagra and scurvy.

Atrophy of the stomach weakens the perception of hunger and victims of starvation are often too weak to sense thirst and become dehydrated. Movements become painful due to the deterioration of muscles and dry, cracked skin caused by severe dehydration. With a weakened body, diseases are commonplace. Fungi, for example, often grow under the esophagus making swallowing unbearably painful.

The energy deficiency inherent in starvation causes fatigue and renders the victim apathetic over time. As starvation progresses, the person becomes too weak to move or eat and their interaction with the surrounding world diminishes. The inability to fight off diseases is often the primary cause of death, rather than starvation itself.

The nights were especially long for Frank. Sometimes he felt that he just couldn't go on. There were times he thought that if he could take his own life, he would. He prayed everyday, saying the Rosary twice each day, using his knuckles to count off each repetition of the prayers. Being a man of faith, he believed that the power of prayer would help him survive. Reciting the prayers over and over was a form of meditation that gave him a brief reprieve from the pain, hunger and disease that gripped his body in an ever tightening vise. Praying kept at bay the crippling doubt that he would ever get out alive. He needed every ounce of resolve he could muster to stay focused on simple survival. Above all he had to keep his wits about him, alert to any opportunity that could bring him an extra morsel of food or sip of water.

"Because I was so thin I developed large blue spots on my ankles, knees, hips and other joints from sleeping on the hard

floor. There was no way to help this and they slowly broke the skin and caused sores. The rice that came through an open slot in the door was always wormy. In the beginning I would pick them out with chopsticks, later I realized that this was the only protein I would get and I stopped picking them out. I had learned to use chopsticks on the way to Saigon but was beaten for using them left handed. Apparently at that time there were no left handed Japanese."

"The guards were not all bad. One was from a dairy farm (which was rare in pre-war Japan) and was homesick. He would try to talk to me but he had little English and I had only the most rudimentary Japanese. Another guard had unusual aquiline facial features for a Japanese and we called him 'The Arab'. There was one guard who always hit us."

The Home Front

Frank's mother and father were notified on the 16th of January, 1945 that he had been shot down over Indochina. Officially, he was listed as M.I.A. (missing in action). The military gave them no further information. It goes without saying his mother and father and his family were devastated by the news. They received a telegram from the Army informing them he was missing in action.

Upon learning that Frank was missing in action, Eva began writing to the families of the other men in his crew, attempting to find information regarding what had happened after the crash. None of the families knew any more than she did, but writing helped her feel like she was doing something. Poignant letters sent back and forth were sincere and heartfelt. They tried to console each other about their sons' unknown fates and did their best to bolster each others spirits, consistently keeping a positive tone in their correspondence.

Some of the crew were rescued within a few days to several weeks, and made it back to China. The families of the crewmen who made it back wrote Eva and told her what little they knew, unable to give her real details because the military strictly censored the mail.

On February 9th, Eva received a letter written by Everett Clark, telling her what he could about the crash and subsequent bail-out. The letter is co-signed by the other returned crewmen.

Lt. E. A. Clark 0-716358
373 Bomb Sqdn. 308 Bomb Grp.
N.P.O 430 c/o Pm N.Y.C.

Dear Mr. and Mrs. Padgett,

This is just a brief note to let you know what we can about Frank. You have probably already been informed about anything that we can say here, but we thought you might like to hear from us.

When we were forced to bail out we all jumped within a short time of each other. Everyone landed safely and we were fortunate enough to get back in a relatively brief time. We haven't heard from Frank or the other boys since.

We realize then this isn't much information but it is all we are able to give you now (due to military secrecy).

All of us extend our deepest sympathy to you, for we know how anxious you must be about Frank. We earnestly hope to have word from him or that he will be able to get back to his base soon.

Very sincerely,

Everett Clark
Harry W. Sherer
Robert W. Smith
John J. Webster
Joseph P. Medon
William D. Sanderson

Eva received their letter with the outward calm she was so good at showing those around her. Inside, it was another matter. Frank was her only child and she missed him dearly and prayed continually for his return. She understood the men of Frank's crew could only give her the information military censors let pass, though it made it no easier for her to bear. Subsequently, Eva and David received a letter from Frank's commander, General Claire Chennault, informing them that Frank was MIA and expressing his condolences.

HEADQUARTERS FOURTEENTH AIR FORCE
A.P.O. 627, C/O POSTMASTER
NEW YORK CITY, NEW YORK
February 16, 1945

Dear Mr. Padgett,

It is with deep regret that I must inform you that your son, Second Lieutenant Frank D. Padgett, has been missing in action since January 1, 1945. No doubt you have already been informed by the war department.

Lieutenant Padgett was Co-Pilot of an airplane which ran out of gasoline while returning from an important sea sweep mission within enemy territory. The crew parachuted from the airplane and while some have returned safely, nothing further has been heard from your son. Every possible effort has been and will continue to be made to locate him, but his disappearance for over a month without word from any of our sources of information, viewed in the light of our experience in this area, leaves little basis for optimism.

Your son will always be remembered by many of his friends and comrades among both officers and men. His cheerful devotion to duty made the task of being a good soldier easier for those who worked at his side. You have every reason to be proud of his contribution to our efforts against the enemy.

I wish to take this means of expressing to you and other members of the family, the sympathy of the officers and men of my command.

Sincerely your,

C.L. CHENNAULT
Major General, U.S.A.
Commanding.

It is impossible to fathom the anguish his parents must have felt when the letter from General Chennault arrived. The letter was empathetic but brutally frank as he holds out little hope for Frank's survival and gives scant details about the circumstances of his disappearance. The general did not encourage false hopes because he knew the odds of Frank surviving were not good. Frank's father, David, was deeply affected by the news that his son was missing. He was frail and the news that Frank was MIA took a heavy toll on him. His mother, Eva, did not despair and continued to believe he was alive and would return home safely.

Erratic treatment was common in many Japanese prisoner of war camps, especially in the ones run by the Kempeitai. Camps run by the Imperial Army usually had a professional army officer in charge and the guards followed some kind of standard that nominally recognized some rights of the prisoners. The Kempeitai camps and jails were run by Japanese military intelligence who considered Americans less than human. They followed a pseudo code that they said was the "Way of the Warrior" or Bushido. This code was used by the Kempeitai to justify the brutalization and torture of prisoners in the name of the Emperor. Many of the Kempeitai were depraved criminal thugs who treated prisoners like animals. There are many horrifying examples of unspeakable atrocities carried out in camps run by these men. Frank, Brach and Gottschall were lucky because they were under the protection of the Hanoi colonel's chop. Instead of more torture, they were simply left to die in their cells from inadequate nourishment and no medical help. Their wounds festered and the diseases they had contracted raged on inside their bodies unimpeded.

"About once a month we were allowed to shower and to brush our teeth with a hog bristle tooth brush. All three of us used the same brush with Jingans Semi-Toothpaste, a can of some

kind of abrasive mint flavored powder. Once they cut our hair and shaved us."

Frank was not able to exercise in any way because there was a rule that prisoners must sit still, day and night. Once a day they were taken out to empty their waste buckets. Although he barely had strength to do it, emptying his waste bucket allowed him to stand, stretch and walk a bit. It was a chance to escape the sickening stench of the cell and have a precious few minutes to breathe fresh air.

In early March, Japanese forces were redeployed around many of the main French garrison towns, and on the 9th of March 1945, the Japanese delivered an ultimatum for the French troops to disarm. Those who refused were massacred. In Saigon, senior Japanese officers invited the French commanders to a banquet. The officers who attended were arrested and almost all were killed. In Saigon the two senior Vichy officials, General Emile-René Lemonnier and Resident Camille Auphalle, were executed by decapitation, after refusing to sign surrender documents. The French upcountry garrisons fared better, however, and, under the leadership of Major-General Marcel Alessandri, a column of 5,700 French troops, including many French Foreign Legionnaires fought its way through to Nationalist China. Martin Windrow "The Last Valley"

"After several months spent recovering from their leg wounds, Frank's crewmates Hugh Pope and George Uhrine were taken by ambulance from Lanessan Hospital to the Citadelle in Hanoi, and then to the Foreign Legion camp at Mont Ba Vi, about thirty miles southwest of Hanoi. Their escape from the hospital happened right before a Japanese detachment searched the hospital for them. When Pope and Uhrine arrived at Mont Ba Vi, there was a group of six American flyers waiting there. They were from Naval Task Force 38 and had been shot down over Saigon on January 12th, 1945."

"Despite being alerted about the March 9th attack, the 7th Legion Company, 2nd Battalion, 5th Foreign Legion Regiment which was guarding Pope, Uhrine and the Task Force 38 men, did not leave Ba Vi until the next day, March 10th. The Legion company divided into three groups, with the Americans in the last group. Unfortunately, since Sergeant Uhrine's broken ankle prevented him from marching, the other Americans were forced to leave him behind. One of the Americans, Red Fetzer, recalled, "It was a dog-eat-dog situation. It was a question of saving the seven of us or all of us being captured or killed."

"The 7th Company headed for the French airbase at Tong, unaware that its parent unit, the 2nd Battalion, 5th Foreign Legion Regiment, had already left the area. By 10:00 p.m., the 7th Company was within a few miles of Tong near a small village

called My Khé when the lead group walked into a Japanese ambush. The legionnaires "were pretty much sitting ducks" one of the Americans, Lynch, recalled as he and the others watched the attack from a distance. In the wake of the attack, a French Sergeant Chef, Jean Günther, suddenly appeared and took charge of the Americans and led them to safety across the Black River where they joined up with the 2nd Battalion. The battalion took Pope and the six Task Force 38 flyers to Son La and a truck carried them to Dien Bien Phu, 250 miles Northwest of Hanoi, where they waited four days for foul weather to clear before a C-47 picked them up and flew them to safety in Kunming."

Some of the French Foreign Legion garrisons, especially in the north, were given a wide berth when they finally surrendered. The Japanese did not want to provoke them into escaping and forming a new resistance army. The Japanese knew what a formidable opponent the French Foreign Legion could be on a level playing field. Because the French leadership had been caught totally off guard when the Japanese attacked on March 9th, the French army was subdued fairly quickly.

French Foreign Legion commandos surrender

March 9, 1945 was Frank's twenty second birthday, though he had very little to celebrate this year. The days, weeks and months of captivity dragged by in slow and painful succession, as his body shrank and his health deteriorated. He was no longer able to eat all of his rice and sometimes lapsed into fevered dreams that mercifully provided temporary escape from grim and painful reality. Some days, Frank came around a bit and was able to eat, but the effects of starvation and disease were becoming unbearable.

After being left behind because of his injuries, "Bobcat" sergeant George Uhrine was later picked up by a Foreign Legion sergeant who tried to save the crippled American by taking him to China on horseback. On March 29th, they had reached Ban Pa Hon in the Hoang Lien Mountain Range, but the next morning both men were captured by the Japanese near the Chinese border, almost within sight of safety. Uhrine was posing as a Hungarian Legionnaire, hoping to escape execution as an American flyer. He and the French Foreign Legion sergeant who had been trying to save him, were taken to Hanoi and imprisoned in the "Hanoi Hilton". Sergeant Uhrine was liberated shortly after the war ended.

Chapter Twelve - French Camp

The world is a dangerous place, not because of those who do evil, but because of those who look on and do nothing. *Albert Einstein*

"On June 1, they took us to the barracks of the 5th Colonial Artillery Regiment. We sat all day in an office, and then they took us back to the Kempeitai jail and put us in our cells. We were confused by this because we thought they were taking us to a new camp but instead, they brought us back. I think that was the low point of the whole experience for me. However, one of the guards, the Arab I think, told me that we would be sent to a prison camp soon."

The news that they would be moved lifted their spirits, though Frank was now so sick and emaciated, he could hardly walk. The diseases he had contracted, the starvation rations and the unsanitary conditions had merged together into a perfect storm of illness pushing him to the brink. Even though he was young and strong when he was captured, the extremely harsh conditions in the Cholon Kempeitai jail had him fighting for his life. During the terrible months of hardship, he kept praying that he would survive the ordeal and make it back home.

"On June 8th, they took us out of our cells. They gave me my wallet and my wristwatch strap with a Japanese wristwatch they substituted for my Air Force issue. I signed for them.

174

They put us in a car and drove us into Saigon to what I learned was the former barracks of the Onzième Infantrie Coloniale (11th Colonial Infantry Regiment). It was called 'Martin des Pallières', who I suppose was a French hero."

Onzième Infantrie Coloniale - circa 1900's

"They took us to an empty three story building and put us in a large bare room with a shower stall in the corner, a wooden table, some benches and wooden cabinets. The guards took Brach and Gottschall away for awhile, and they returned carrying two saw-horses and three planks. These were set up as a bed for me because I was an officer. They gave us tatami mats, blankets, rice husk pillows, bars of soap, safety razors with blades and three toothbrushes. The rest of the building was empty. A nearby building housed Indochinese soldiers who had been in the French army. The entrance to our building was guarded. We could walk the corridors but not get out. They brought us a dinner of cooked rice with pineapple and some teriyaki meat. A guard threw in a bunch of bananas. I was suffering from beriberi and could barely hobble around so I was very grateful for these. The benjo (toilet) was in the back of the building and we were accompanied by a guard whenever we had to go. After dark, I had an attack of dysentery and went to the benjo accompanied by the guard who had given us the bananas. At bayonet point he relieved me of my watch."

"The next morning they set up a desk in front of the building and a civilian in a white suit read a lengthy document in Japanese which he then translated into English. The document said that we were prisoners of war and would be treated properly but executed if we tried to escape. We had to sign a pledge not to escape which was easy. We were 1200 miles from the nearest friendly forces, there were no Caucasians except for some civilian French in Saigon and certainly, no 6'3" people at all. Because of the beriberi, I could barely walk 50 yards and I was down to 115 pounds. I was a mess. I looked like a walking skeleton. My legs and arms were sticks and my hip bones stuck out at right angles. Skin hung from my chest, the muscles atrophied and my ribs were bare bones. When I signed, the man in white told me I would be paid the salary of a 2nd lieutenant in Japan. I asked about overseas pay but he said since I was captured in Indochina, I was not entitled to overseas pay. I signed a payroll book and they gave me some Indochinese piastres. It was obvious that the money was intended to be given to the guards to bring us things from the outside."

"The man asked me if I had any complaints. At first, I said no because I was uneasy about telling him about the guard stealing my watch. I figured the guard might retaliate. I decided that if I didn't say something and they saw the guard with the watch, they might think I tried to bribe him and I would be punished. I told the man in white about it. He was furious and a discussion with the Japanese officers followed. The civilian said they would rectify the matter, it was not supposed to happen. We were taken back to our room and in a few minutes, a guard brought my watch back. Later, I saw the guard who had taken it from me being marched away at bayonet point. We never saw him again. I think they simply took him out and shot him."

"The next day the Vietnamese prisoners in the camp were moved out of the nearby barracks and columns of French prisoners of war began to arrive. The French filled up the barracks and took over food preparation. The French were not supposed to talk to us or we to them. They of course paid no attention to this rule and neither did we."

" I was finally out of the Kempeitai jail and in an environment where I could begin to look at myself and my condition. I had survived the deprivation and the starvation but I was sick and needed help. I was suffering from beriberi and knew that I needed vitamins badly. The Japanese guards took money from me and brought back peanuts and fish oil capsules. The French gave me limes, which I ate whole, skin and all. As time went by, we got other fruit with our rations and I slowly began to feel better. After the French arrived, one of them brought me a bundle wrapped in newspaper. Inside was a pound or so of what appeared to be lumps of dried gray mud. He said to swallow a spoonful every morning with tea. Apparently, the dried mud was opium and it stopped the runs. I still had the disease, but the symptoms were greatly lessened. For malaria the French gave me quinine."

Soon after this, two American Navy flyers, Quinn and Grady, were brought into the camp. They had been crewmen on a PBM (seaplane) which had engine trouble and landed along the coast near Vung Tau. They sent out their maydays and were told that there was an American submarine on its way to pick them up. As the sub arrived though, a Japanese patrol came upon the scene and the Navy flyers were forced to flee inland.

Members of the French resistance led them away from the coast and into the mountains. After days of hiking, they made it to an abandoned French outpost near Pleiku and hid there along with the three Frenchmen. They were betrayed to a Japanese platoon by a local Vietnamese sergeant. A firefight with the Japanese ensued. During the gun battle, an American and several Frenchmen were killed. There were a number of Japanese killed during the attack but they eventually prevailed, taking the rest of the Americans prisoner. That night, the Americans were positioned around a fire, their hands tied behind their backs. The Japanese commander paced back and forth, interrogating them in broken French and Japanese, trying to find out who they were and how they got there. He grew more and more enraged because they remained silent.

Suddenly, without warning, the Japanese began to drag the men away, one by one. Shouting and screaming, they were dragged out and shot. Quinn tried to get up but was hit in the back of the neck with a rifle butt, knocking him out. After seven of the American prisoners had been killed, the executions suddenly stopped, leaving two Americans still alive.

Quinn and Grady, the two survivors, were paraded along the main street of Kontum. Leading the procession was the victorious Japanese platoon followed by stretchers bearing six of their own KIA's. The Americans, bound at the hands and elbows, were convenient targets for rocks hurled at them by the populace. Quinn and Grady were then tortured and questioned for days about the identities of underground members and then consigned to a Saigon POW camp. The Japanese platoon commander, who had directed the executions of the PBM crew, was himself executed as a war criminal after the war.

Ensigns Grady and Quinn were brought to the Martin des Pallières prison camp where Frank and his crewmates were. Grady was deathly ill with malaria. The French camp doctor gave him a quinine shot. Unfortunately the needle was old and it broke off inside of his hip causing severe pain. The quinine worked and he recovered, although the needle had to be surgically removed after the war. For the story of Quinn and Grady, see Appendices C.

"Every morning we got a pot of tea, some rice and half a duck egg apiece. We were now five, so sometimes we got three eggs and others only two. The French hardboiled them but I asked for raw eggs and just swigged those down or made omelettes using the ovens. Some mornings the tea tasted different and we sat around pleasantly dazed after drinking it. The French said it was made with the husk of some nut that I was unfamiliar with. The French had given me a French lieutenant's uniform and a mosquito net for my plank bed. This proved a godsend as my four crewmates came down with Dengue fever. There was no treatment for Dengue and they were ill for several weeks."

Rumors began circulating around POW camps that the Japanese High Command had issued orders to all Camp Commandants that in the event of an Allied invasion of Japanese-occupied territory, prisoners of war were to be exterminated in whatever way most convenient. This news came from the underground networks or friendly guards who talked with the prisoners. There were elements in the Kempeitai who imagined themselves to be the true descendants of Samurai warriors. If Japan were to be defeated, they would go down fighting, taking as many prisoners with them as possible. The Americans were bombing Saigon heavily and word was out that the allies were close to Japan. Anything might happen. In such a fluid environment, the prisoners believed that it was possible that these orders would be carried out.

If bad things began to happen, being imprisoned with the French was a timely and fortunate thing for the Americans, especially because Frank spoke French. The French knew the countryside and the civilian underground. They were armed and had good intelligence and they could escape the prison if it became necessary. Being on good terms with the French gave Frank and his men a little extra edge if things began to deteriorate.

The new camp felt like a "land of plenty" to the Americans. For five months they had been deprived of everything. While in the Kempetai jail they had no clothing except for a loincloth. No food except for rice with worms and maybe a bit of vegetable. No medicine of any kind if they were ill. No contact with anyone. That might have been the worst of it all, not knowing what was happening outside of the prison walls. They had no idea how the war was going and it was not easy for them to keep up their hopes up of getting out alive. Now, they were in a camp with a lot of French soldiers and civilians and since Frank spoke French, they were treated with dignity. Frank was nursed back from the brink by the French. They gave him food and medicine and made sure that he and is men were not harassed by the Japanese guards.

"The Onzième Infantrie had a library in the barracks prior to the Japanese takeover and it was still around. All the books were written in French. I got some history books about the Balkan wars of 1911-13 and I read to the other Americans. There were also a few copies of the magazine published in Shanghai by a German. It was patterned after National Geographic and filled with propaganda. It was named 20th Century. It had good pictures and after having had nothing to read and being locked up for so long, it was a way to pass the time."

"About the third or fourth day, a French Commandant (major) came by and told me that since I was here, I might as well get something out of the experience. He told me to come to a certain room in another barracks in an hour. When I got

there, a group of French officers and I sat around and talked. I went over there on a regular basis and we discussed anything and everything."

Frank's ability to speak and read French opened a social door to his French counterparts. He spent many days with them and got to know some of them well.

"The French Army in Indochina had been loyal to Marshall Petain and his puppet Vichy government. They were nominal allies of the Japanese and now that the tide had shifted, all of them were Cross of Lorraine and American allies. The French Army drafts priests as ordinary soldiers. There were no chaplains and the Japanese didn't permit religious services, but most evenings one of the priest-soldiers would conduct a short service exposing the Sacrament. The priests who were drafted into service were defrocked until their service was over. They were not allowed to give communion".

"One day, I was summoned to the building where the French generals were quartered to play bridge with them. We used cards with only dots on them, no numbers. The suits in French are Pique, Coeur, Carat and Tref. For example, a five of hearts had the heart symbol and four dots. After the game, one of the Frenchmen opened a large trunk and handed me a large packet of piastres for which I signed."

"I used my money to get rum, anisette, moon cakes and other things we needed from the guards. With the money I got from the French generals and the pay from the Japanese, we could start living like human beings. There were some real characters among the French. There were two half Vietnamese officers who were twins. Their mother was a princess of some city and their father a French civil servant. One looked Caucasian and the other Vietnamese. There was Joe Tchakalian who had been stationed in the pre-war French Concession in Shanghai. He spoke French, English, Russian and a Shanghai dialect of Chinese. He was a short, wide guy who was always smiling and talking about sex. There was a Foreign Legion regiment containing a couple of Australians. There were a couple of officers who spoke English with an Aussie accent. It turned out they had grown up in New Caledonia and went to Australia for the equivalent of high school."

"My lower wisdom tooth got infected. The French soldier who was the nominal doctor/dentist sat me in a chair. I was held down and my mouth forced open. The dentist then took a white hot poker and cauterized the gums around the tooth. It wasn't particularly painful but the stench of burning flesh is unforgettable."

"The French used other techniques to treat medical cases when they had no western medications. Usually these treatments were based on traditional Chinese medicine. One was for a severe chest problem, cold or pneumonia. The French doctors had 6 to 8 glass cups in which they would put a few drops of grain alcohol, allowing it to vaporize which it did quickly in Saigon's hot climate. They lit the fumes with a match, inverted the cups and put them on the back of the patient. The flame caused the flesh and skin beneath the cups to be drawn up into the cups. This would increase the circulation in that area and leave a circular bruise where the cups were placed, but it seemed to clear the chest congestion."

"The French were able to get some green coffee beans. They roasted the beans in a steel drum mounted on a stand rotating over an open fire. They ground the beans and gave us the ground coffee. One of the articles of clothing given to me by the French was a pair of ragged shorts. I cut out one of the pockets and sewed it to a heavy wire loop with a handle. I would put the grounds in the pocket and drop it into a pot of boiling water to make coffee. This arrangement allowed us to use the grounds twice. Where there was a will, there was a way. Men who have little learn to make do with little."

"Eventually there were 4,500 French and 5 Americans in the camp. One was Ray Natua who was half Tahitian, one quarter

American and one quarter French. He had been a petty officer radioman in the French Navy stationed at Dalat in the Central Highlands. Ray was anti-French in his sentiments. Every morning there was a long line waiting to get into the latrine house. Inside, the pits were a seething mass of maggots. The French customarily shook hands with their friends when they first saw them in the morning, so the guys coming out would shake hands with those in the waiting line. Ray refused to do this. He would say in French, 'I would rather shake hands with your prick, it's probably cleaner".

"The rice in prison camp was the red un-hulled type rather than the white rice in the Kempeitai jail. The red rice was wormy but undoubtedly better for us. The white variety was what the Japanese Army ate. The French always started the midday and evening meals with soup. It was often thin, just a few wisps of vegetable such as sweet potatoes and various cabbages. Sometimes there was a little meat or fish, including canned tuna called 'thon' in French. We always had 'nuoc mam', a Vietnamese fish sauce. We sprinkled it liberally over our rice. It smelled a little unpleasant but tasted good and salty. It probably was a good source of the vitamins and minerals I needed so desperately."

"The French told me of many other American aviators captured by the Japanese and executed. Being the only

American who spoke French, I decided to start writing down each one and recording whatever information I could get. This became possible when the Japanese returned my possessions, among them my fountain pen. Paper was hard to come by but I gathered up small pages and slips whenever I could. Each time I heard one of these reports, I tried to get as much information as I could: place, time, date, the number of airmen and their names. Then I wrote down each incident on one of the scraps of paper and tucked it back in my belt. Eventually, I had 30 or 40 of these incidents written down. I wasn't sure I would survive the war myself, but I felt a responsibility to bear witness to the fate of these men. If I had died over there, I would hope that someone would do the same for me."

"The French officers wore a belly band of felt or wool. They claimed it helped control intestinal problems to which European derived Caucasians are susceptible in the tropics. They gave me one and I wore it, hoping it would help me as I was still having problems with the dysentery. It did seem to help and so I wore it all of the time. It was quite wide and we all wore them folded over once or twice. It served another purpose. The fold is where I kept the slips of paper with the information I had recorded about the American flyers. I had to be very careful because to get caught with this information would have been fatal. I always wrote them up in the evening when no one was watching."

As the Japanese continued to lose ground in the Pacific, they began worrying about the consequences should the allies find out about the torture and atrocities carried out on allied flyers. Immediately following the March 9, 1945 coup, when the Japanese took away control of Indochina from the French, the Japanese began executing American flyers wherever they were captured. This new policy continued until the surrender on August 15, 1945.

"The French had several radio receivers, one that I saw was built into a large diameter section of bamboo and was disguised as a water container. Because of the receivers, we generally knew what was going on in the war. There was a French foreign language newspaper printed in Saigon and copies sometimes found their way into the camp. It was passed around until it would get unreadable. It then had an equally important function in the latrines."

"There was an older French lieutenant named Bombier who had been a non-com for many years before being fully commissioned as an officer during the war. He spoke no English but was a great rumor monger and came around every day to talk with me. Prison camps are full of rumors about everything imaginable and Bombier was the 'horses mouth' of many in our camp. He told me that he was sure that the French generals would work out a 'modus vivendi' with the Japanese

to allow the French to go back to their garrisons and things would go on as they had before the March 9th overthrow when the Japanese had attacked the French after they noticed the French clearing long flat strips in the jungle and heard tunneling noises under some of their installations. I gave little credence to Bombier's stories and neither did his fellow officers. This story was not believable because the French were no longer Vichy meaning they were no longer Japan's ally. The overthrow on March 9th left many French officers dead, executed by the Japanese. Resentment was seething throughout the French Army and civilian population. To send the French back to their garrisons would be like releasing an enemy force directly into the heart of the Japanese Army of Indochina."

"On June 12, 1945, a group of B-24s from the 7th Air Force flying out of the Philippines made a bombing raid on Saigon. We all dove into the slit trenches and listened as the bombs whistled down on the Saigon docks. One of the B-24s was hit by anti aircraft fire and was trailing smoke from one engine. We didn't see any parachutes or hear anything and hoped that it somehow limped home. We were some distance from the docks so weren't in too much danger from the heavy bombing that was occurring as the allies tightened the noose around the Japanese. Later, I learned the fate of the bomber and its crew."

"On August 9, 1945, Bombier walked in and said *'François, qu'est ce que la bombe atomique?'* 'J'ai dit Bombier, il est un grande secret.' I said this because I had read the famous 1938 article in Liberty Magazine about the theoretical possibility that an atomic bomb could be made. I asked 'Bombier, pourquoi vous demande a moi qu'est ce que la bombe atomique?' He said *'Il a dit parce que on a tombe sur Japon'.* 'Bombier, j aidé fit la guerre c'est fini'." The French with access to their secret radios soon confirmed what Bombier had said. Within a few days the Japanese were seeking peace. At first, we were hesitant to believe what we had heard. I felt like I had been there for many years. The non-stop struggle to survive had made time irrelevant. Time was measured by bowls of rice, when would you get the next one and would there be a scrap of something a little more nutritious in it? Suddenly, here was news the war might be over, really over. Thoughts of the world around us began working their way back to the surface but we dared not hope too much, in case the news turned out to be false. Still, maybe this time, it might be real and we'd make it out of here alive."

"Our hopes were confirmed on the morning of the 15th or 16th, the Imperial Rescript, the Emperor's message telling his subjects of the unconditional surrender to the allies, was read. We watched as the guards assembled in front of their quarters. The camp commandant read them the Rescript. One of the

guards unsuccessfully tried to break his sword over his knee."

The Imperial Rescript was the first time any person outside of the Imperial Court had ever heard the Emperor's voice. He spoke using the language of the Imperial Court which the commoners could not understand. Many were confused by the fact that he spoke with the voice of a human being. Up until this time, the Emperor was considered a god in Japan.

In Japan itself, public reaction to the Emperor's speech varied. Many Japanese simply listened to it, then went on with their lives. Some Army and Navy officers chose seppuku (disemboweling) over surrender. At a base north of Nagasaki, Japanese Army officers, enraged at the prospect of surrender, pulled 16 captured American airmen out of the base prison and hacked them to death with swords.

"That evening we were called out for our twice daily roll call. In the first rank were the five Americans. Next to us were the men from a garrison named 'Fleur Le Merht' which had held out for a more than a week against the Japanese takeover in March of 1945."

"The main reason they were able to hold out for so long was because one French sergeant, who looked a lot like Harpo Marx, had gone out at night with a truck and picked up a

couple of cases of 'Sten' guns (similar to an Israeli Uzi' but more primitive) which an allied plane had air dropped to him. He drove back to the garrison to find that the Japanese were attacking the fort. He persuaded the Japanese to let him and the truck back through to talk his comrades into surrendering. The Japanese thought his cargo consisted of only regular supplies. But the garrison, now rearmed with brand new Sten guns, was able to hold out for a few more weeks. Unfortunately, many French paid a high price for their insolence and were executed after surrendering."

"As we stood in line for roll call that day, the Japanese began the usual 'Bango!', meaning count-off in Japanese. We American prisoners from the Kempeitai jail, dutifully said 'Ichi, ni, san, shi, go' (one, two, three, four, five). But when the guard ordered 'Bango' to the first French Fleur Le Merht garrison man, they called out in unison, 'Un, deux, trois, quatre'. The guard said 'Mata, mata.' (wait, wait), 'Bango en Japonais' (Count off in Japanese). From the middle of the line the Marx brother double looked at the guard, drawing his finger in a slashing motion across his throat saying, 'Eh, la guerre c'est fini.' (The war is over. This will be your fate.). The guard turned and walked away and a half hour later, the guard was seen pedaling out of the gate with his possessions rolled up in a tatami mat strapped on his rear fender. That was our last roll call"

192

"Gaetan Faure, a French civilian businessman came to see me the next day. He had been in the Kempeitai jail for some weeks awaiting execution for running an underground resistance group in Saigon, but he was released into our camp. He told me of the fate of two American flyer's who were there at the same time he was. Their plane had been hit by ground fire while bombing the docks in Saigon and they were the only ones able to bail out before the plane had crashed. Gaetan was able to whisper to one of them and get his name. Unfortunately, he could not get the name of the other flyer. There was nothing he could do to help them except to bear witness to their last few days of life. He said that the two Americans were beaten and tortured for five days to the point they were unrecognizable."

"They were then taken out and executed by beheading and their bodies dumped in an unmarked grave. I added the Americans names and fates to my list and then hid it away in my waist belt."

DIS LA VERITE

"…et bastonnade sont les procèdes ordinaires d'investigation", *Copyright 1947,*
G.H.P.

Frank himself had been tortured in Hanoi, and although not as
grave, he never the less had an idea of what the two flyers had
gone through before their horrific deaths. He was sickened by the
savage brutality the Kempetai rained down on the helpless men.
He knew that if it wasn't for the Hanoi colonel's chop on his
papers, he and Brach and Gottschall would have met this same
fate.

194

EVEUX SPONTANES

"...Asphyxie par l'absorption d'eau.." *Copyright 1947, G.H.P.*

The name of the American flyer Gaetan Faure told Frank about was Allan Nicks. The other American flyer's name was Joseph A. DeMaria. He and Alan Nicks had been waist gunners in a B-24 bomber, #44-42329, that went down over Saigon on June 12, 1945. This was the bomber Frank had seen that same day. It was hit by antiaircraft fire and he saw it flying away with black smoke pouring out of one of its engines. The plane went down 40 miles NNW of Saigon. Sgt. Nicks from Texas and Sgt. DeMaria from Massachusetts, were the only ones able to bail out of the crippled aircraft. They were with the 7th Air Force, 380th Bomb Group, 529th Squadron flying out of Murtha Strip in the Philippines.

THE EMPORIA GAZETTE
Tuesday, August 6, 1946

Executioner Hanged - Tokyo. Aug. 6 (AP)—Sunio Tomono, a member of Japan's dreaded "thought police", has been hanged for beheading two American fliers. The announcement was received today from the Southeast Asia command at Singapore. The Americans were identified as Sgt. Allen Nicks and T-Sgt. Joseph A. DeMaria. addresses unknown, whose B-24 crashed near Cholon, French Indo-China June 12, 1945." The two, only survivors taken prisoner, were beheaded by Tomono the following month.

The actual transcript from the war crimes trial of Sunio Tomono taken from the Singapore Straight Times, located in Appendices B.

UNE SUITE D'INTERROATOIRE

"…On se contenta de la sortir dans le couloir ou il agonisa sans soins."

"That weekend the Japanese announced that there would be

an open air mass just inside the main gate. The mass was to be

said by a French priest from the Saigon cathedral. The day before, the priest came to hear confessions, in case the Japanese decided to slaughter us. Four of us five Americans were Catholic but I was the only one who spoke French. The priest refused to hear the confessions of my other three countrymen as he spoke no English and refused to allow me to translate for the other three. So none of us went to confession or the mass."

Many prisoners worried about the Japanese intentions. The war was over but the Japanese were still in control of the camp and the prisoners had an uneasy feeling. They heard the rumors about the extermination order to be carried out if Japan was invaded. It is remarkable that when they at last had the chance to go to confession and mass, they all decided to forfeit the chance because the priest had denied the non-French speakers. To a Catholic, this was giving up what might be the last chance to reconcile with God. It speaks powerfully of the bonds of unity and loyalty that developed among the American prisoners.

In other POW camps, the Japanese made preparations for mass executions. POWs in Burma were ordered to dig large tank traps around the perimeter of the camp. While speculating on the reason for the traps, one of the POWs voiced the thought in everyone's minds - the tank traps looked remarkably like mass graves, said Ex-POW, Fred Seiker. In some places friendly guards offered an apology as they warned POWs of the impending executions. Ex-POW, Tom Wright, confirmed "They (Japanese) told us that they were sorry, but they were going to have to shoot us." Why the majority of POW commandants did not carry out the execution orders was not clear. *POW-WWII.com*

"A day later, the Japanese allowed the French to meet with their families and friends who were civilians. They cordoned off the street in front of the main gate for this purpose. Since we had no relatives or friends, we stayed in our quarters. A Frenchman came in and said that there was someone at the gate asking for us. It was an Irish Brother who had come to apologize for the French priest. The brother took us across the street to the Shell building and up to the office of the head of Shell in Saigon. We were given clothes, a drink and some food. The brother took us out the back door of the building and we were FREE! We went to a house several blocks away where a Dutchman who had escaped and was passing for a French civilian, lived. We were sitting on his veranda, drinking beer and eating bananas when along came the Japanese prison camp doctor. The doctor stopped and motioned for us to come along and follow him back to camp."

"After the surrender, three more American aviators were brought to the French civilian hospital in Saigon. They were in bad shape. One had a wound infested with maggots which a

Japanese soldier picked out with a pair of chopsticks."

"The Japanese had a huge flock of ducks that they kept in pens within the camp. The ducks provided eggs for the guards and occasionally for prisoners. Each day the guards and some French prisoners would herd the ducks down to a park in central Saigon where there were large freshwater ponds. The ducks would feed and swim in the ponds and at the end of the day were herded back to the camp. The day after we had "escaped", we noticed the French duck herders boiling large pots of water and plucking the ducks that they had killed. That evening we had duck soup and boiled duck for dinner."

"One day at about dusk, a French prisoner came for me and took me to another building which overlooked the guards' quarters. On the veranda leading to the third floor bay, which was directly above the guards' quarters, sat a scrawny little Frenchman with a white gauze mask over his mouth and nose."

The Japanese guards were very much afraid of Tuberculosis and the French led the guards to believe that this man had Tuberculosis. The guards would never set foot in the bay. The French prisoners living in the bay had a radio attached to the underside of their table. They also had a storage cabinet filled with guns and grenades. The French said if the Japanese tried to kill all the prisoners, the French would make sure to take as many Japanese with them as possible."

"A couple days later, they called me over to see if I thought we Americans would like a *gamelle* (a pot in the French mess kit) of roast pork with gravy for lunch the next day. Trying to keep myself from shouting YES, I quietly said sure, but asked where was it going to come from? There were several men there including my new friend Gaetan Faure. The French explained that one of the men, who stood 6'4" and was heavily muscled, was going to go over the 6' high fence that surrounded the pen where the Japanese kept the pigs and goats. His name was Pierre and he was to get a kid goat the French doctors wanted for the sick patients in the camp infirmary. The French said that he might also grab a pig while he was at it. Pierre had a large, sharp knife. He intended to go over the fence, cut the throats of the kid and the pig, throw them on his shoulders and scramble back over the fence. Pierre had been a butcher in the French Army but had killed another soldier by mistake. He was in the French military jail when the Japanese had taken over. It sounded like a great plan and Pierre seemed to be just the man to do the job. The Frenchmen had some anisette so we had a drink to the success of the operation and I went back to our quarters."

"The next day the aroma of roasting pork wafted through the camp. I can tell you that it set my mouth watering. At noon, the gamelle filled with hot roasted pork and gravy, along with a pot of rice, was delivered. I hadn't told the other Americans what had happened the previous night, but when they smelled the roasting meat, I told them that we would be having some for lunch. When it came, the four of us (Grady was still very ill but recovering from Malaria in the camp infirmary) sat down and had a lunch like no lunch we ever had in our lives."

"A day or two later, the Japanese colonel in charge of the camp had us moved to more spacious quarters in a room with a window overlooking the street in back of the camp. They also gave me a hospital bed with a mattress and told me that I would now be treated as a Japanese officer of equivalent rank. This meant the guards had to salute me and I was supposed to return the salute. I asked the colonel when I would receive the sword a Japanese officer wore. He and he said it would take several days to draw it from central supplies. Needless to say, I never got the sword."

"The colonel came to inspect us in our new quarters and it so happened that Ray Natua was there.
The colonel counted 'Ichi, Ni, San, Shi, Go, Roku. Roku?'
Frank, Brach, Gottschall, Quinn, Grady ???
Ray Natua quickly said 'Me houseboy. Sweep up.'

The colonel said 'Ah, juto.' (Oh, good) and, hands behind his back, he walked away".

"Ray had a friend in Saigon, a large, fat, half Cambodian who looked like 'Fat Boy' in the comic strip 'Terry and the Pirates'. Ray somehow got in touch with him and the friend appeared in the street below our window with a large canister of ice cream. We hauled the canister up to our room with a rope. We could get rum and anisette through the guards and used overripe pineapples and raisins to make 'swipe' in a canvas bag we hung on the wall."

"We thought we would soon be free and several of the French officers invited me to go to a plantation one of them owned in the jungle to hunt tigers and elephants after liberation. They also said there would be several beautiful young women along but it was never to be."

Chapter Thirteen - British, Dutch & American Camp

All the great things are simple, and many can be expressed in a single word: freedom, justice, honor, duty, mercy, hope. *Winston Churchill*

"Around the 25th of August, the Japanese informed me we were to be transferred to the British, Dutch and American camp. Most of the Americans in the camp had been prisoners for a number of years. They were captured on Java or when the cruiser "Houston" was sunk off Java at the beginning of the war. The Japanese were releasing Red Cross supplies to the camp. The 198 Americans had no officers and were complaining about the division of the supplies. At this time I was thinking in French, wearing a French lieutenant's uniform and was suspicious about the intentions for the transfer, especially since Gaetan had told me of the fate of Alan Nicks and his fellow crewman. Afraid the Japanese had become aware of the information I had gathered and that we would be made to simply disappear between the two camps, I said we would go only if several French prisoners rode on the truck with us. My reasoning was that if the French prisoners didn't come back, there would eventually be an investigation, but if we simply disappeared, no one would miss us. After a day or so of negotiations, the Japanese agreed. We said our goodbyes to the Frenchmen, Gaetan gave me his address on Rue Dalat in Saigon and we got in the truck and drove across town to the other camp. It was located on the Rue Jean Eudel in the

Cinquieme Artilleres barracks where we had been briefly on June 1st when it was a camp for French prisoners."

"We arrived safely. Quinn and I were taken straight to the British officers' quarters. There were four surviving British officers, all doctors. No line officers were left among the British, although there were a number of Dutch officers remaining. Quinn was older than I and probably had an earlier commission date, but for some reason I was in charge, perhaps because that was the way it had been in the French camp."

"After introductions had been made, the senior British officer said 'We were unsure who to get to bat for you but fortunately an American sergeant has volunteered.' The British had been prisoners for over two and a half years but the officers still had batmen who brought them their meals, washed and pressed their clothes and acted as valets. Of course the American Army had no such thing for anyone under the rank of general, but I didn't demur. I knew that I was probably the youngest American prisoner, but they put me in charge. The Americans in the camps were all five or more years older than me and I knew nothing about them. I figured the sergeant who had volunteered to bat for me knew the set up and fellow prisoners, and was probably an operator who could give me the information and advice I was going to need. He did. As for his duties as batman, he simply copied his British counterparts."

"As in the French camp, we lived in a large bay with mattresses and mosquito nets. On the verandah outside the bay, there was a large earthen pot called a 'dong' which was filled with water. Each morning, I would strip down to my skivvies and my batman would throw buckets of cold water on me. I soaped up and he would throw more cold water over me. Saigon is hot, but at dawn there is a chill and it was a brisk awakening. I had accumulated a couple pairs of shorts and two shirts by then. After my bath from the dong, I would put on the laundered and pressed clothes laid out by my batman. He would then bring me my breakfast tray. The cooking was done by Indonesian prisoners who were part of the Dutch army. We had Indonesian curry with lots of red pepper flakes floating in it three times a day. The Dutch said it kept intestinal parasites in control and was the only way they had been able to survive all those years in Indonesia."

"A few days after we were transferred it was Queen Juliana's birthday. The Dutch officers had a dinner to which the British, American and Japanese officers were invited. We all sat on the floor of a large room with low tables in front of us and were served by Indonesians. The meal consisted of the famous Indonesian Rijsttafel, rice and garnishes brought one by one. It wasn't an elaborate dinner but it was an example of how prisoners kept their dignity in the face of adversity, following long held traditions. At the end, toasts were proposed by the officers. When it came to the Japanese officers' turns, I heard banzais for the first time. I was astonished at the camaraderie the professional British and Dutch officers displayed towards the Japanese and vice-versa."

"The flip side of this was when a 19 year old British major and his Ghurka corporal orderly appeared one day at the front gate of the camp. The major and his orderly had been dropped into Saigon the night before. He had been dropping behind enemy lines during clandestine operations since he was 16 years old. He summoned the Japanese colonel in charge of the camp. The major told the colonel what his orders were. The Japanese colonel leaned nonchalantly against a gate post listening. When the British major finished, he did an about-face and marched off, then the Ghurka corporal (they are from Nepal, carry long knives and look Japanese) stepped forward and knocked the colonel on his ass saying 'When you talk to a British officer, stand at attention.' The Ghurka then turned and walked away."

"By now the amoebic dysentery was really bothering me and restricting my physical activities. However, after the British major incident, prisoners began to go freely out of the camp. One morning, my batman told me that three Americans had gone to the center of the city, gotten drunk and were in the city jail. I had to go get them. I took my batman and Gottschall and started walking into the city. About noon we came to Rue Dalat unexpectedly and came to the number of Gaetan's house. I didn't know Gaetan had gotten out of the French camp. I thought I would tell his family that I had been with Gaetan recently and he had been okay when I last saw him."

" I knocked and his wife Simone came to the door. Simone told me Gaetan had gotten out of the camp and was on a business errand but would be home in a few minutes. We went in and while we waited, she gave us each a glass of ice with orange liqueur which we sat sipping until he arrived. Gaetan insisted we stay for lunch and had the amah prepare some turkey and rice."

"While we were eating, gunfire broke out on the street outside. Two factions of Vietnamese were fighting. It was the beginning of what became the Vietnam War. A road block had been set up in the street, bullets were whizzing about and we all dove to the floor. The house was made of stucco or stone and the window sills were high so we were able to move about crouching down. The fighting continued through the afternoon but after dark, it started to slow down. We went upstairs where there were enough bedrooms to accommodate everyone."

This was the beginning of what historians call the "First Vietnam War". It would continue until the Viet Minh defeated the French at Dien Bien Phu in 1954.

"Gaetan's house was joined to the other houses on the block by walls. It was in a compound with a garden in the center. The roadblock stayed up for three days and because I was wearing a French uniform, it wasn't safe to go outside. The French families in the compound had a number of children, some of them teenagers. Gaetan's daughter Brigitte was 11 years old. On Sunday, someone got out a phonograph and there was some dancing in the garden-courtyard. The Indochinese servants in the house were able to go out and get food, but Caucasians stayed inside the compound."

"On Monday, the roadblock was gone and the gunfire stopped. I went downstairs and outside. Everything was quiet. The men I had come to help had been released from the jail earlier. I went to the hospital, found the Americans there and arranged for them to go back to the camp. Then I went back to camp. That day or the next, I was told I was to go and meet a colonel at the Hotel Continental. This colonel was an OSS officer who had been dropped in to Saigon along with his sergeant."

"The first Americans into Saigon entered by parachute on 1 September 1945. They were a prisoner-of-war evacuation group under First Lieutenant Emile R. Counasse. This was an advance element of Operation Embankment, in turn planned as early as 10 August by OSS Detachment 404 based in Sri Lanka (Ceylon). The above group was to accompany British troops to Saigon with the stated objective of investigating war crimes, locating and assisting Allied POWs, particularly Americans, securing American properties, and tracking political trends.

Operation Embankment was commanded by Lieutenant Colonel A. Peter Dewey, who arrived in Saigon by C-47 on 2 September with four team members landing on a Japanese airfield near the main Saigon (Tan Son Nhut) airport. Dewey was told that he was on his own and could expect no logistical help from the British. Eventually, the OSS team liberated 214 Americans held in Japanese POW camps outside of Saigon. The majority had been captured in Java and employed on the River Kwai railroad before being interned in Saigon. Another eight were airmen shot down over Indochina." Geoff Gunn, *"Origins of the American War in Vietnam: The OSS Role in Saigon in 1945."*

"I walked back downtown and reported to the Colonel. I turned over to him all of the names that I had collected and kept hidden in my waist band. I felt a burden lifted as I handed them over. The Colonel told me that he wanted me to work

with his sergeant in setting up the evacuation of American prisoners. For some reason my memory during those days is hazy, perhaps because of my illness. The sergeant set up radio transmitters on the roof of the building across the street from the Continental, level with the room we were working out of. I don't remember sleeping there, but I remember the beds had lace coverlets on them. I remember one day Andre, a French officer I had come to know well, came by with his beautiful French mistress. I think we had lunch in the hotel. The Italian consul came and asked to be evacuated with his family and staff. There was also a 13 man Filipino swing band, caught while on tour in Saigon. They wanted to be evacuated and we agreed, although we were going to Calcutta in India, the opposite direction from the Philippines. My impression is that the Colonel kept me at the Continental, but I have no recollection of when, if ever, I went back to camp."

By now, Frank's illnesses and his weight loss caught up with him. He was sick, tired and running out of gas. Despite his poor physical condition, he followed the Colonel Dewey's orders and went back to the British, Dutch and American camp to organize the Americans there into groups and got them to the airport in Saigon for the evacuation.

"Finally, on September 6th I believe, the C-47's arrived at the Saigon airport. There were medical people on board, doctors and nurses. They loaded us on and we flew to Bangkok for refueling. Thailand had been a nominal Japanese ally during the war but apparently the Caucasian civilians had not been interned. At any rate, it was a hot afternoon when we arrived and the British ladies had set up some card tables and were serving hot tea. The Brits were firm believers in following tradition and customs. They did not let a war get in the way of their beloved tea at noon. From Bangkok we flew to Rangoon where we re-fueled again and then flew on to Calcutta. During this last leg, I had a severe attack of dysentery and was so weak that I had to be taken from the airport to the 142nd General Field Hospital on a stretcher in an ambulance. I think by this time the day was almost over."

"The next day we were issued some clothing, some back pay and I was officially promoted to first lieutenant. There was then a rule that every commissioned officer who had been a prisoner for more than 90 days was to be promoted one rank. I didn't know it but I was up for promotion when we went down so I had really been a first lieutenant in January. If I had known this, I would have made captain in Calcutta and eventually discharged a major rather than a captain."

"In the Calcutta hospital they caught all of us up on our immunization shots: cholera, yellow fever, the works. Of course in my weakened condition my system reacted with a raging fever which triggered an attack of malaria. First the sweats, then the chills and uncontrollable shaking. I was given a shot of quinine and I think of morphine."

"I missed lunch and dinner and the attack stopped around midnight. One of the nurses went a block or so up the road to an Indian restaurant and brought me back some chicken and a couple of bottles of beer and it was delicious and I felt much better."

"The next morning I awoke feeling okay and after breakfast I went out in the garden next to our ward. In the garden were little stalls and vendors selling all kinds of things. I bought a pair of mosquito boots from one of them and when an Indian with a pad of telegraph blanks came by, I bought one of them and sent a telegram to my parents saying 'Am whole, sound. Send home news. Frank'. I was concerned about my father's health and I did not want to tell them I was ill. He was 65 and I did not want to worry him. Unfortunately, there was no way for my parents to reply, but the cable that I sent from Calcutta was the first news that my parents had that I was alive. They did not receive the Army's official cable until three days later."

"I stayed in the hospital in Calcutta for several days. While I was there, the orderlies would come around and collect our urine samples in old beer bottles. One guy had put a half empty bottle of real beer under his bed the night before and somehow it had been collected. This caused a considerable amount of consternation when the results came back from the lab. In addition to the Saigon prisoners, there were some from Singapore and some left from the Rangoon jail. I wasn't up to much sightseeing but I think I might have gone to a nearby restaurant to get some dinner once."

"After a few days in the Calcutta hospital, I got orders to fly to Karachi. The flight clear across the sub-continent is a very long one. I think we stopped for re-fuelling in New Delhi. By now, I was feeling much better. At Karachi, I was quartered on the base while waiting for a flight back to the states. At that time, the Army Air Force had the world's longest and fastest airline in the world. It was called the Red Ball Express running from Karachi to New York using C-54's (DC4). After a couple of days in Karachi, I was informed that I would be flying out on the Red Ball Express with a full load of ex POW's and I would be the officer responsible for the passengers, making sure they indeed got home to America."

"I conducted a roll call beside the plane in Karachi, got my people on board and we flew to Bahrain. We re-fuelled, ate at a mess hall on the base, re-boarded and headed for Cairo. Again we re-fuelled and ate and then flew on to Casablanca. Here, we finally had an eight hour layover and they took us to a military

VIP hotel on a hill, had a very good meal and were assigned rooms."

"I was very tired and assumed the others were, too, so I lay down to sleep. My sleep was soon interrupted when someone came running in to tell me there was a commotion involving some of my people and a WAC in the hotel. I couldn't find out what was really going on, so I had the WAC removed and sent the men involved in the ruckus to their rooms with orders to stay there until I sent for them. At the end of the day, we were bussed to the airport, boarded another C-54 and flew on to Santa Maria in the Azores, landing there at night. Again we ate and re-fuelled and then flew across the Atlantic to Gander, Newfoundland and then on to New York."

"I was sent to Santini Hospital somewhere in New York. Each bed had a telephone and although it was late, I called home and spoke to both of my parents. I was transferred the next day to Halloran General Hospital on Staten Island and after extensive blood tests they found that I had amoebic dysentery. I was suffering from severe headaches each afternoon. These had started in the Kempeitai jail and continued every day. I was sent on to Moore General Hospital in Ashville, North Carolina. It was a tropical disease medical center and they were experienced treating all the various strains we had picked up in the Far East. After a few months, I was sent home to

recuperate. I was in and out of the hospital for quite awhile after this and eventually released and sent to Greensboro, South Carolina and Fort McPherson outside of Atlanta where I was discharged as a captain in March of 1946."

The War is Over

All of the crewmen of the B-24 Liberator named the "Bobcat" survived the war. Seven of them made it back to China, some quickly, others were moved around the countryside by the French underground until they could be smuggled back to their base in China. Frank, Brach, Gottschall and Sergeant Uhrine did not make it home until the end of the war. Frank and his two crewmates, Brach and Gottschall, were liberated on September 6, 1945 after more than eight months in captivity. Uhrine and the French Legionnaire acting as his guide were captured by the Japanese on March 29, 1945 while attempting to cross the border to safety in China. Sergeant Uhrine, knowing his best chance for survival was to avoid identification as an American flyer, managed to convince his captors that he was a Hungarian Legionnaire. He was imprisoned in "the Hanoi Hilton" with other Legion prisoners until the end of the war.

The Japanese surrendered on August 15, 1945, and supposedly all combat ceased. There were several instances in Japan where prison guards, upon learning of the surrender, beat and then executed their American captives. This did not happen in Saigon. There,

American prisoners of war continued to be held in the camps until the British, under General Gracey and the Americans under Colonel Dewey, arrived in Saigon and arranged for their evacuation.

The first objective for both the British and American advance teams (under Gracey and Dewey) was to make sure the Japanese were disarmed. Next, they went to the camps where the allied prisoners were being held and impressed upon the Japanese that they had better take proper care of their prisoners. The Japanese forces in Saigon were eager to appease the victors and released supplies from the Red Cross and allowed French civilians to bring in food and other supplies. The British also directed the Japanese to hold the prisoners in camp for their safety until enough aircraft could be assembled for their evacuation from Saigon. It was three weeks from the surrender before six C-47's landed near Tan Son Nhut Airport to pick up the American prisoners. Frank and all of the American prisoners of war in Saigon were flown out of Saigon on September 6, 1945.

Archival sources make no mention of Colonel Dewey's brief to investigate Japanese war crimes, indeed these records possibly remain classified. Setting aside high profile cases, such as with Field Marshal Terauchi Hisaichi, it was the French who vigorously prosecuted Japanese war crimes in Vietnam, of which there were many against French officials and French and

Vietnamese civilians alike. French investigations led to the execution of five Japanese for the murder of American airmen downed in Indochina. Many Japanese, Kempeitai included, avoided investigation by throwing in their lot with the Viet Minh as military advisors and in other roles. Geoff Gunn, "Origins of the American War in Vietnam: The OSS Role in Saigon in 1945."

The whereabouts of the list of airmen that Frank had compiled and turned over to Colonel Dewey remains a mystery. It is likely that the list was turned over to American intelligence and used in the war crimes tribunals after the war.

The overall death rate for POW's in Japanese camps was a staggering 27.1%, seven times that of POWs under the Germans and Italians. The death rate of Chinese was much larger. In these camps, prisoners were hardly given any food to eat and most were forced to work in inhumane conditions. The prisoners were disease-ridden, starved, tortured and sometimes executed. In one incidence, 61,000 Prisoners of War were forced to work on the Burma-Thailand Railway in the most atrocious conditions over 12 months, where approximately 13,000 POWs died.

The American public largely ignored the war crimes trials that took place in Tokyo and throughout Asia in 1946-1948. Unlike the charismatic Nazi leadership, who were infamous throughout Europe, the Japanese leadership was not well known. Japan's crimes against Asian peoples had never been a major issue in the postwar United States, and with the notable exceptions of former U.S. prisoners of war held by the Japanese, even remembrance of Japanese wartime atrocities against Americans dimmed as years passed. That was due in part to the Allied propaganda, which did not want to criminalize the Emperor. If the Allied public saw him as a criminal, they would demand his removal, which would have prolonged the war.

The French held their own war crimes tribunals and tried many Japanese for crimes against humanity. Many of the men convicted were sentenced to death. This illustration, from a book "La Kempetai", is of the men who were found guilty by the French war crimes tribunal and sentenced to be hanged.

1 commandant Tanita Burichi ; 2 capitaine Ichikawa Shigeru ; 3 lieutenant Kuwahata Tsugio ; 4 sergent Sasa Kuniyoshi ; 5 adjudant Sumimoto Shigeru ; 6, sergent Oda Susumu ; 7 sergent Yokomizo Kichinosuke ; 8, gendarme Kano Toshisada.

As Frank and his fellow prisoners of war left Saigon, French Indochina was about to erupt, as old rivalries between the Viet Minh and the French exploded again. America under Roosevelt did not want to see the French back in control of Indochina. The British wanted the opposite, feeling that if Indochina fell to a nationalist movement like Ho Chi Minh's, British ruled India might be next. General Gracey, seeing that he was undermanned and losing control of the situation, armed recently liberated French soldiers, hoping that they could help keep things under control. This did not happen. The French immediately went after the Viet Minh and attacked and killed many civilian Vietnamese. The Viet Minh organized a general strike shutting down all commerce, electricity and water supplies in Saigon.

On the 28th of September, Major Peter A. Dewey, commander of OSS Detachment 404 and close relative of the Republican Governor of New York, Thomas Dewey, who would run for the presidency against Harry Truman in 1948, was shot and killed in an ambush, apparently by Viet Minh who mistook him for a Frenchman. He had been forbidden to fly the American flag on his jeep by the British General Gracey, who considered the OSS and Americans as meddlers. Dewey, as he drove through Saigon, blundered into the ambush in an unmarked jeep and was shot dead. He was the first American casualty of the Vietnam war. Just before

219

his death, Dewey had filed a report on the deepening crisis in Vietnam, stating: **"Cochinchina is burning, the French and the British are finished here, and we ought to clear out of Southeast Asia."**

Chapter Fourteen - Full Circle

"Whatever America hopes to bring to pass in the world must first come to pass in the heart of America." *Dwight D. Eisenhower*

Honolulu, Territory of Hawaii - December 1949

The courtroom was quiet as the tall, thin young man rushed in carrying a large briefcase. He was rather pale, with dark hair and a boyish face, wearing a blue suit and a wide, unusual looking tie. He walked directly to the Defense table, shaking hands with each of the men seated there. His clients were members of Kotohira Jinsha, a Shinto shrine dedicated to a Japanese Sea God. The shrine was located in Kalihi Valley on the island of Oahu in the Territory of Hawaii. The bailiff asked all to rise as Judge Frank McLaughlin came in and called the court to order.

Just moments before, the young man had been a block away at the Aliiolani Hale, the Supreme Court Building where the Chief Justice of the Hawaii Supreme Court had sworn him in as a licensed attorney and a member of the Hawaii Bar Association. This would be his first case as a practicing attorney and like everything else he did, he wanted to win it.

As he hurried down the sidewalk to the Federal Court building, the young lawyer from Vincennes Indiana reflected on the path his life had taken. Just five years ago, he had been a prisoner of war fighting to survive. Now here he was, living in Hawaii with a growing family and a new career, something impossible to imagine while he was imprisoned. He was very grateful to have survived the war, he knew many who had not.

He felt himself free from any loathing or bitterness towards any man. He was no longer angry about being held and abused as a prisoner of war. The war was over and the men who had held him were no longer part of his life. It would be a waste to give any time to resentment for what was already done. Maybe it was his faith, possibly his intellect which told him that life was too short for grudges. He didn't know. He had chosen to live in Hawaii, a place where people of many cultures and ethnic backgrounds got along together. It didn't have much to do with what you looked like or where you came from, it had more to do with what kind of person you were. He believed the past was the past and looking towards the future was a much better way to live. The now is gone almost before it has time to be present. The idea to live life well today made sense. Knowing that it could be gone before even being counted snapped him back to the present. He was late and this was a very important day for him.

The case involved the seizure and sale of the Kotohira Jinsha property by the federal government on the grounds that the Shinto religion was "enemy tainted" and associated with emperor worship. World War Two was over, but the fear of enemy aliens and the paranoia that went with it were still fresh in the minds of many Americans.

The young man with the boyish face had fought in the war and knew first hand the fear and bitterness that war creates. His experiences had opened his eyes to the good and bad on both sides. He knew the difference between those who make war and those who are sent to fight in it. Not long before, he had been held as a prisoner by men who looked very much like the men he was representing that day. However, his clients were Americans, protected by the U.S. Constitution and he was there to defend their rights.

Kotohira Jinsha

"An eye for an eye only ends up making the whole world blind." *M.K. Gandhi*

Upon graduation from Harvard law school in 1948, Frank had accepted a job with a well known Honolulu law firm and moved to Hawaii with his family. He had to wait until the end of 1949 to take the Hawaii Bar exam because of Hawaii's one year residency requirement. He passed the exam at the top of his group for that year and on November 29, 1949, was sworn in as a licensed attorney and member of the Hawaii Bar Association. Frank didn't have much time to celebrate after the ceremony as he was already due in court that very day to try his first case.

The courtroom was quiet as he walked in. He knew he was late, but it couldn't be helped. He quickly walked to the table where his clients were sitting and shook hands with each of them. These men were respected members of the Japanese community in Hawaii. Frank was a relative newcomer and this was his first case as a practicing attorney. He felt he had done his homework well, finding a point of law that would stymie the government attorney.

The case involved the seizure of the Kotohira Jinsha temple by the federal government's Alien Property Custodian in June of 1948 and the subsequent attempt to sell the property in 1949. Before the start of World War II, the temple, a Shinto shrine, had been a thriving and vital center of worship, cultural activities and social gatherings for the Japanese community surrounding around it. The shrine was a place of worship to the sea god Konpira-san. After the Japanese attack on Pearl Harbor, the U.S. government viewed this shrine and all other Shinto shrines as suspect because it associated the religion with emperor worship and Japanese nationalism. The head priest of the temple, Rev. Masao Isobe, was arrested and interned on the mainland. Later in the war, Isobe was repatriated back to Japan.

During the war the congregation was still allowed limited cultural activities at the shrine, but martial law and the fear of internment made people wary and apprehensive. Afraid to go there and participate, they no longer saw their shrine as a place of refuge, but rather a place of potential danger. Many in the Japanese community had been arrested after the start of World War II and sent to internment camps on the mainland. In December of 1947, despite the absence of a priest, members of Kotohira Jinsha began trying to restore religious worship at the shrine. However, they faced another crisis on June 1, 1948, when federal officers raided the shrine under the "Trading with the Enemy Act". Their property was seized by the federal government on the grounds that the Shinto religion was enemy tainted and associated with emperor worship.

On March 4, 1949, an announcement for the sale of the Kotohira Jinsha property by the government appeared in local newspapers. Kotohira Jinsha hired Frank's law firm Robertson, Castle and Anthony to represent them. Frank, as the junior man in the firm, was assigned the case. It was considered un-winnable by the senior members of the firm because they had recently lost a case very similar to this one. The senior partners may also have been concerned that anti-Japanese sentiment in the community could influence proceedings, preventing them from winning.

On March 31, 1949 Kotohira Jinsha filed a lawsuit against the Attorney General's office for misusing Section 9 of the Trading with the Enemy Act against a civilian organization not under the influence of the Japanese government. On November 29, Frank, who had just been admitted into the Hawaii Bar that morning, petitioned the court to restore the shrine to Kotohira Jinsha. The government attorneys argued that the Shinto creed was a Japanese cult and not a true religion. But they forgot to file the required oath of verification. Frank caught the omission and the judge ruled against the government, but gave them time to come up with the signed document. This was a positive start for the case showing that justice was possible for those willing to fight for it.

"The Kotohira Jinsha members were hopeful and confident all the way through. They believed that justice was going to be done, that they were going to get their shrine back. It was idealistic, but they really believed. I never saw any indication from them that they had any doubts about it."

The story was picked up nationally by the Associated Press. It was considered a landmark legal case at the time and it made the papers throughout the country. See Appendices E for the full story.

The actual trial began on March 27, 1950. During the trial, Jujiro Koto, a World War I veteran, testified that Kotohira members did not pray to the Japanese emperor, nor for the success of Japanese military operations. "The Japanese government didn't commit even a penny for our shrine here" said Tarokichi Hiromatsu. "It is an individual right to believe in your own religion. The Constitution says we have that right."

The case was decided in Federal Court on May 18, 1950. Padgett argued that the government had not followed proper procedure when they seized the temple and the judge agreed. Contrary to the senior partners' predictions, Federal Judge Frank McLaughlin ruled against the government and the land was released back to the members of the Kotohira Jinsha community.

In his ruling, Judge McLaughlin found the Attorney General's office in violation of the First Amendment rights of plaintiffs in the United States Constitution with reference to Robert H. Jackson in American Communications Association v. Douds. Judge McLaughlin found the Attorney General's office had no basis on which to exercise the Trading with the Enemy Act, moreover, since 1945 Japan had abolished state religion under Douglas MacArthur and by judicial order returned seized property to Kotohira Jinsha. *Kotohira Jinsha v. McGrath, 90 F. Supp. 892 - Dist. Court, D. Hawaii 1950 (1950)*

Frank and Kotohira Jinsha members 1950

A portion of Judge McLaughlin's opinion:

We have not yet come to the point, nor will we ever while "this Court sits", where the Government can take away a person's property because it does not approve of what that person believes in or teaches by way of religion or philosophy of life. The First Amendment forbids it generally, and the dissenting portion of Mr. Justice Jackson's opinion wherein as to a similar proposition he states:

"Efforts to weed erroneous beliefs from the minds of men have always been supported by the argument which the Court invokes today, that beliefs are springs to action, that evil thoughts tend to become forbidden deeds."

Probably so. But if power to forbid acts includes power to forbid contemplating them, then the power of government over beliefs is as unlimited as its power over conduct and the way is open to force disclosure of attitudes on all manner of social, economic, moral and political issues.

"These suggestions may be discounted as fanciful and farfetched. But we must not forget that in our country are evangelists and zealots of many different political economic and religious persuasions whose fanatical conviction is that all thought is divinely classified into two kinds, that which is their own and that which is false and dangerous. Our protection against all kinds of fanatics and extremists lies not in their forbearance but in the limitations of our Constitution."

This vesting did unduly infringe a freedom protected by the First Amendment, and the plaintiff has proven itself eligible under the Act to have a judicial order directing the Custodian to return to it the vested property. And it will be so ordered formally when Findings of Fact and Conclusions of Law are settled upon notice.
Federal Judge Frank McLaughlin

The ruling revitalized the Kotohira Jinsha. More importantly, it set a precedent in protecting the property and religious freedoms of Shinto shrines throughout the country. Despite the ruling, Justice Padgett recognizes that similar injustices could happen again. **"I would hope not, but...... it could happen again, if we had another war with a large immigrant population here with a lot of assets."** Said Padgett. **"It probably would happen again."** *Mark Santoki, The Hawaii Herald* **January 1, 1992**

Frank's words were prophetic. In 2010, a Muslim religious group requested that they be allowed to build a mosque and community center near "Ground Zero" in New York City. The project named

229

"Park 51" was to be built two blocks away from the actual site of the September 11, 2001 attack in which Islamic fanatics crashed fully loaded commercial passenger jets into the World Trade Center killing over 3000 people. Some have made comparisons between the September 11th attack and the Pearl Harbor attack in 1941. The thought that a Muslim mosque would be built near "Ground Zero" enraged some who blamed all Muslims for the September 11th attack. The controversy renewed interest in the Kotohira Jinsha case. The First Amendment questions raised by Kotohira Jinsha vs. McGrath, were thought by some to have similarities to the "Park 51" controversy. Both cases involved the exclusion of the rights of a religious group to gather and worship on property they owned. A full transcript of the Kotohira Jinsha decision by Judge Frank C, McLaughlin can be found on the internet at:

http://www.leagle.com/xmlResult.aspx?page=1&xmldoc=195098290FSupp892 _1775.xml&docbase=CSLWAR1-1950-1985&SizeDisp=7

Frank went on to become a successful attorney in Hawaii continuing with the law firm of Robertson, Castle & Anthony for a number of years before starting his own law firm, Padgett, Greeley, Marumoto and Akinaka. In 1980, he was appointed to the Hawaii Intermediate Court of Appeals and in 1982, he became an Associate Justice on the Hawaii Supreme Court. He served for ten years before retiring in 1992.

Frank on Hawaii Supreme Court

Frank has said many times he has lived a charmed life and that things just always seemed to go his way. I am always surprised when he says this because his early life was anything but easy. Luck certainly had something to do with his survival when he was shot down. The one in a million chance of crossing paths with the colonel in Hanoi who had gone to Harvard and whose chop likely followed him through the months of imprisonment, protecting him from execution, might even be attributed to divine intervention. Enduring those long months of captivity while being starved to death, though, had much more to do with strength, courage and indomitable will, rather than mere luck. His survival had to do with a quality that is all too rare these days, that is, the ability to find common ground.

Epilogue

When Johnny comes marching home again hurrah, hurrah
When Johnny comes marching home again hurrah, hurrah
The men will cheer and the boys will shout
The ladies they will all turn out
And we'll all feel gay
When Johnny comes marching home.
Patrick Gilmore

On September 5, 1945, after more than eight months of being held as a prisoner of war, Frank was liberated. He and over 200 other American prisoners of war were flown out of Saigon on C-47 aircraft. On his way home, while in a military hospital in Karachi, he found a man selling telegraph forms. He bought one from the man but because there was a character limit, his cryptic message to his mother and father said:

AM WHOLE SOUND - SEND HOME NEWS - LOVE = FRANK PADGETT.

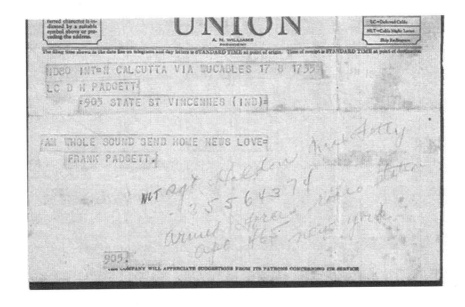

This was the first news Frank was alive. His parents had kept their hopes and spirits up as best they could over the long months he had been MIA. David and Eva couldn't believe their eyes when the telegraph came. Right out of the blue, a message from Frank, telling them that he was alive and well! It was the miracle they had prayed for and they celebrated, thanking God for giving them back their son. Imagine, the war was over and they hadn't heard from Frank for over eight months. They knew he had been shot down over enemy held territory. They had been told by his crewmates, the ones that had made it back to friendly lines, that after bailing out, Frank had landed safely but from there, nothing else was known. Now, eight long months later here was a telegram from Frank himself telling them that all was well. He was safe, sound and coming home.

"Finally, I was sent home by way of Bahrain in the Persian Gulf, Cairo, Casablanca, Santa Maria in the Azores, Gander and finally New York. We landed in New York on September 13th, 1945."

He was sent to Santini Hospital in New York where he called home for the first time and spoke to his parents. Transferred the next day to Halloran General Hospital on Staten Island, he was officially diagnosed with amoebic dysentery. He was transferred by military hospital train to Moore General Hospital in Ashville,

234

North Carolina. Military hospital trains had nurses and doctors assigned to each car with beds lining the windows and Frank slept most of the trip. Moore General Hospital was a tropical disease center. It's staff was experienced in treating the various strains of diseases troops had picked up in the Far East. Frank was there for treatment on and off for the next 6 months. While he was in the hospital recovering, he met a pretty nurse from Georgia. He said "She was so nice and always trying to make me comfortable." Her name was Sibyl Pharr. She was a 2nd lieutenant from Dacula, Georgia, a small town outside of Atlanta.

After an initial stay at Moore General of about a month, Frank was given an 85 day leave to go home to see his folks. He took a train from the hospital to Vincennes, Indiana where he stayed with his mother and father. He was there a few weeks when he got a call from Everett Clark, his navigator from the "Bobcat". Clark had just been discharged from the service and was driving across the country to his home in Springfield, Massachusetts. Clark asked Frank if he wanted to go along. Along the way, they could stop in Pittsburgh to see Bill Gottschall. Frank accepted and they set out on a road trip along the back roads of Indiana and Pennsylvania to Pittsburgh where they stopped at Gottschall's home. Together for the first time since they had been liberated, the three men had much to catch up on. Frank and Everett stayed with Bill's family for a couple of days, continuing to their final destination in Massachusetts. When they arrived at Clark's home, the family invited Frank to stay awhile. He agreed and stayed with them for a few days, but feeling that the family needed some time to themselves, Frank took a bus to New York.

He checked in to the Biltmore Hotel in Manhattan and called a few friends of his from Harvard. There was a big dance being held Saturday night at the Plaza Hotel, so Frank made plans to meet up with them at the Plaza. While he was out on the dance floor with his date, another couple brushed by them. Over the sound of the orchestra, Frank heard his name called out. He turned, and dancing next to them was a pilot he recognized from Luliang. The guy was in one of the other B-24's in his squadron. He was standing there looking at Frank in total disbelief and loudly exclaimed **"Frank Padgett. What the ##*!" are you doing? You're supposed to be dead!"** They burst out laughing and grabbed a table reminiscing about their lives since China, about how large the world really was now that they had seen a bit of it.

After New York, Frank took a train back to Vincennes where he stayed for a couple of weeks, finishing his leave. He then went back to Moore General in North Carolina to await new orders. He was very happy to see Sibyl again and they resumed dating. It was during that time that their relationship started to get serious.

Sibyl and Frank married on January 25, 1946. The ceremony was held in the hospital chapel. Sibyl was given away by General

Logan, the commanding officer at Moore General Hospital. Frank was friends with the general and they often played bridge together. For their honeymoon, Frank and Sibyl were sent to Miami Florida with all expenses paid by the Armed Forces newspaper. The Army wanted a big story about a wounded soldier living better due to the good care that the Army medical services were giving him. The honeymoon couple stayed in an officers' hotel for ten days and went deep sea fishing on the Air Force's yacht. They went to the races, were wined and dined nightly and had a great time.

After the war. Off to honeymoon in Miami.

Returning to Moore General, they lived off base in a rented house and waited until Sibyl was discharged from the Army. During this time, Frank applied for admission to the Harvard School of Law in Massachusetts and was awaiting placement. As soon as Sibyl was discharged, they went to Fort McPherson outside of Atlanta for Frank's Terminal Discharge. When they were done, they drove up to Dacula, Sibyl's home town outside of Atlanta for a short stay with her family. Finally, they took a train up the eastern seaboard to Boston to await the start of Frank's first semester at Harvard Law School.

"I entered Harvard Law School in June of 1946. I was receiving a 30% disability payment from the government, which came out to $95.00 a month and the two of us lived on this while I went to school. It was a tough couple of years and we compounded the tight finances by having two children during this time. Our first son David was born in January, 1947 and our first daughter Elizabeth, was born in November of the same year."

During this time, Frank and Sibyl were living in a tiny apartment in Cambridge. They were on such a tight budget that they could only afford meat once a week, that is unless Frank splurged and bought a horse steak. With two children under the age of two, Sibyl stayed at home and cared for them. They didn't have a car, so they walked or took a bus wherever they needed to go. The winters were especially hard and they were living on a shoestring.

In 1948 during his last year at Harvard Law, Frank's father became extremely ill. Some years earlier, probably 1936, David had cut himself while cleaning a rabbit. His knife slipped and cut his hand to the bone. He came down with what seemed to be the common flu with a high fever, chills, headache and sore throat. The symptoms worsened and the doctor diagnosed it as Tularemia, a parasitic infection passed on to humans when they are cut cleaning rabbits. Antibiotics are the treatment of choice for Tularemia now but they were not available back in 1936. People infected with Tularemia had to ride it out until their bodies grew strong enough to beat the infection. Not all made it and many were permanently impaired as it continued to weaken the immune system.

The consequences of Tularemia took their toll on Frank's father. David became very frail and had trouble with his heart. In 1948 he had a stroke that crippled him. He could no longer walk nor could he speak. This all happened very quickly and some of his law clients had court dates scheduled and needed David in court to argue their cases. There was one particular case that could not be postponed or given to another attorney. Frank got a call from his mother asking him to come to Vincennes and help his father. His mother and grandfather A.J. spoke to the Indiana Bar Association, as well as the presiding judge, and permission was granted for Frank to argue the case for his father.

Frank was somewhat familiar with the procedure. He had been arguing cases in Cambridge for needy clients of the Legal Aid society since his first year at Harvard and felt he could do the job for his father. The preliminary work had been done just before his father was struck down by the stroke. Frank's job would be to come up with the closing argument and present it to the court. Frank and Sibyl packed their clothes, bottles and supplies for the children and took the train from Cambridge to Vincennes. Although the circumstances were somber, his family, especially his father, were proud of Frank on that day.

"I graduated from law school in September of 1948. Just before graduation, representatives from law firms from around the country came to the Harvard campus to interview us as prospective employees. I was interviewed by well known East and West Coast firms. A number of them offered me a job. There was the managing partner from a firm in Honolulu, Hawaii. I was interviewed and he offered me a job. I don't know what it was, maybe the war, but I started thinking about his offer. The more I thought about it, the better the idea of living in Hawaii seemed. Northeast winters were brutally cold and the warmth of Hawaii was just too much to resist."

Frank moved to Honolulu in 1948 and Sibyl soon followed with the two eldest children and another on the way. They rented a house beyond Aina Haina in an area named Portlock on the southeastern tip of the island of Oahu. The bungalow they rented was right on the water and this is where Frank began his pursuit of diving and spear fishing. Hawaii was a great place to be in the 50's if you were young and liked the ocean. Frank made friends with other diving enthusiasts and they would go on fishing trips most every weekend. He didn't know it at the time, but his love of the ocean and swimming made him a great mentor to all of his kids. He was a swimmer, body-surfer and diver back when there were very few guys from the mainland doing these things.

He and Sibyl were able to live the idyllic life that Hawaii offered during their early years there.

"Work during the day, small dinner get-togethers in the yard with the ocean out front, a bonfire going and the kids running around down on the beach. Not much to worry about now that the war was over."

Frank's natural instincts, courage, intelligence, wit and a whole lot of luck had helped him survive the brutalities of war, when so many had not been as fortunate. He was a father now with a couple of kids, another on the way and a job that he had aspired to for so many years. He and his family were living in a real paradise in the Pacific and life was good.

Living in Portlock did have a few drawbacks for Frank and Sibyl. One was the lack of a car. Frank would get up every morning and wait for the bus which came by at 5 am. He'd get off in downtown Honolulu and walk to his office, right off of Bishop Street.

Honolulu was a beautiful little city located on the south side of the island of Oahu, sitting at the base of the Koolau Mountain Range, with Diamond Head to the east and Pearl Harbor to the west. In the main downtown area, stately old stone buildings of colonial style lined the main streets. Many of them were the head offices of companies like Castle & Cooke, Alexander & Baldwin , C. Brewer & Co., American Factors and Theo H. Davies & Co.. These five companies were known as the Big Five. The phrase Big Five, evokes visions of post-annexation and pre-WWII Hawaii's political and economic structure, dominated by five companies involved in Hawaii's sugar and pineapple industries.

Bishop Street, Honolulu circa 1950

The Big Five were the dominant economic powers in Hawaii at that time. Attorney general of Hawaii, Edmund Pearson Dole once said, referring to the Big Five, "There is a government in this Territory (T.H.) which is centralized to an extent unknown in the United States, and probably almost as centralized as it was in France under Louis XIV." Boards of Directors of the Big Five companies were made up of members who served on each other's boards and voted almost as one entity. They were Republican and almost exclusively Caucasian. Their political and economic goals were to grow their power and wealth, keeping wages for the immigrant workers low.

Frank came to know many of these men. They were mostly business associates and Frank's firm was a very old and reputable one, with some senior partners having close family ties to the men who worked at or ran the Big Five companies. Frank came from a long line of Democrats and felt and voted as a Democrat. His political views were more aligned with those of the Democratic Party in his new home state and he was active in Party business. Later, he would help draft the political platform of the Democratic Party of Hawaii and his advice was sought out on questions pertaining to legal aspects of Party business.

In 1949, while busy with his work as an attorney and striving to become a partner in the firm he had joined, he started getting feelers from the Air Force. Might he be interested in coming back on active duty? He was in the Air Force Reserves already, keeping his air time current by flying on training missions out of Hickam Air Force Base, near Pearl Harbor. On the first Saturday of each month, Frank drove to Hickam at 5 a.m. in a borrowed car. He and a couple of other reserve officers would get aboard an old DC-3, fly it up to Kona on the Big Island of Hawaii and take on any freight they had. On the way back, they would stop at Kahului on Maui to refuel, then head home. It was a long Saturday for a young man with responsibilities and Frank began thinking about dropping his service commitment. He had a family to think about now and wanted to spend more time with the children.

Frank and Sibyl's third child was a girl and they named her Glen after Frank's paternal grandmother. Glen was born in February of 1950. Right around that time, the Air Force was talking to Frank about ramping up reserve training. This meant the time commitment for him would increase. It was a difficult period, a new child on the one hand, his country needing him on the other. The Air Force wanted to form two air transport squadrons flying DC-4's. One squadron would get trained first and then be based in Japan, the other would stay in Hawaii, train new crews, and then go to Japan to relieve the first squadron. The Korean Peninsula was rapidly heating up and the U.S. wanted to be ready in case the whole thing suddenly blew.

Frank was mulling over the idea of continuing his military commitment when the Korean situation did blow. The Korean War began in June of 1950. The North Koreans came streaming across the 38th parallel and into the South. Southern forces were outnumbered, under-gunned and had no combat aircraft. They fell back, suffering heavy casualties.

The need for experienced pilots was great and Air Force reserve pilots with the training and active flight credentials were the first to go. Next, the Air Force began drafting all of the military trained pilots they could get from civilian airlines around the country. Hawaii of course was subject to the draft and the Hawaiian and Aloha Airlines pilots were some of the first to go.

Frank had never flown a DC-4 and needed training. The Air Force reserve unit he was with was formed into two squadrons and both started ground school with the aircraft. Frank bought a car for the first time and began the training at Hickam. After a couple of weeks of ground school, he was ordered to fly down to Kwajaleien Island with a couple of experienced pilots, giving him some air time in a DC-4. They were flying to Johnson Atoll for fuel before heading on to Kwajaleien. It was nighttime. Once the plane was airborne, the other two pilots handed Frank the controls and he flew the rest of the way to Kwajaleien. It was a sort of "trial by fire" in that it was more than five years since he had flown a four engine plane, much less at night, which required him to land at Kwajaleien on instruments. He recalled it was a bit unnerving. In any case, from Kwajaleien, the plane was heading for Enewetok Atoll and Frank did not have the security clearances necessary to go there. Frank was left there on Kwajaleien as the plane flew on without him. He hitched a ride back to Honolulu on another DC-4 later that day and when he got home, he talked the situation over with Sibyl and decided he had already done his part.

He had gone off to war when called to duty in 1943 and as a bomber pilot, he had flown as many missions as he possibly could. He was shot down and captured by the Japanese and spent the remainder of the war in a prisoner of war camp. It had taken him a long time to recover from the ravages of that hard time. He had a new family now and a new life just beginning. The next morning, he called his commanding officer, and with some regret, informed him he would be retiring from the Air Force.

In time, Frank and Sibyl had six children, four boys and two girls. In 1954, the family moved to the town of Kaneohe on the windward side of the island of Oahu. The family home overlooked Kaneohe Bay and the Marine Corp Air Station. Coincidently, the Air Station had been attacked on December 7th, 1941 at the same time Pearl Harbor was being destroyed and pictures of the attack were taken that day from their house.

My father's friendship with Gaetan Faure continued after the war in the form of letters between the two. In 1956, when my parents began traveling to Europe, Frank and Gaetan were reunited for the first time since the war. On a subsequent trip in 1960, Gaetan gave Frank the book "La Kempetai", an illustrated book that reveals the terrible realities of being a prisoner of the Kempetai. Of all the characters in my father's war stories, Gaetan was the one who really stood out. Whenever my father spoke of him, it was with a kind of reverence, and naturally, my brothers and I picked up on this and Gaetan became a larger than life figure in my imagination. In 1963, I was lucky enough to be taken along on one of my parents' trips. Gaetan invited us to stay at his country estate for several weeks. It was a large old farmhouse located about forty miles outside of Paris overlooking the river Brie. Gaetan had always been a heroic figure to me and I can still remember seeing him for the first time as he came to the gate to greet us. He was not the big, strapping underground fighter I had built in my imagination. He was probably 5'9" with grey hair and very sharp brown eyes. He was friendly, but reserved in the French manner.

He and my father spent many hours talking, but unfortunately I spoke no French so couldn't understand a word of what was said. These two men had a common bond, both had been prisoners of the Kempetai. They had faced and luckily survived an experience that many had not. After our trip, my father and Gaetan continued their friendship, writing letters and meeting every few years. Gaetan continued his import-export business, dividing his time between Paris and Saigon until 1973, two years before Saigon fell to the Communists. Frank continued on with his successful law practice until he was appointed to the Hawaii Intermediate Court of Appeals in 1980. In 1982 he was appointed to the Hawaii Supreme Court, serving until he retired in 1992.

Frank and Sibyl at home, 2005

Frank is now 89. He and Sibyl still live in Hawaii on the island of Oahu and are spending their days among the friends they have known most of their adult lives. Frank has remained a devout Catholic and feels that his faith helped him survive the hardships he endured in life. Frank and Sibyl are still very active in the community and church. Both love to cook and create many memorable dinners. They practice Tai Chi three times a week with the group they belong to.

Frank and Sibyl at Tai Chi practice, Honolulu - 2011

I sometimes take for granted that my parents will be around forever. I will always be thankful for the opportunity to tell my father's story and I'm grateful that both of them have lived so long, as it has given me the chance to really get to know them.

After the War - A Historical Perspective

Japan surrendered on August 15th 1945. In the surrender document signed September 2nd on USS Missouri, it was stipulated that to the north of the 16th degree northern latitude, the Japanese forces should be disarmed by Nationalist Chinese forces, to the south of that line, by the British.

In September 1945, General Sir Douglas Gracey led 20,000 troops of the 20th Indian Division to occupy Saigon. During the Potsdam Conference in July 1945, the Allies had agreed on Britain taking control of Vietnam south of the 16th parallel (then part of French Indochina) from the Japanese occupiers. Meanwhile, Ho Chi Minh proclaimed Vietnamese independence from French rule and major pro-independence and anti-French demonstrations were held in Saigon. Ho Chi Minh was the leader of the communist Viet Minh.

The French, anxious to retain their colony, persuaded Gracey's Commander in Chief, Lord Mountbatten, to authorize Gracey to declare martial law. Fearing a communist takeover of Vietnam, Gracey decided to rearm French citizens who had remained in Saigon. He allowed them to seize control of public buildings from the Viet Minh. In October 1945, as fighting spread throughout the city, Gracey issued guns to the Japanese troops who had surrendered. He used them to help restore order in the city. According to some socialist and communist commentaries, this controversial decision furthered Ho Chi Minh's cause of liberating Vietnam from foreigners' rule and precipitated the First Indochina War. French General Leclerc arrived in Saigon in October 1945 to assume authority but it was not until well into the first half of 1946 that enough French troops had arrived to allow General Gracey to return with his troops to India where 20th Indian Division was disbanded.

The territory was placed under military administration and was handed over to the French in 1946.

Indochina was reorganized, now consisting of the three monarchies Laos, Cambodia and the republic Vietnam. In 1949/1950 they were granted the status of independence within the French Union. French troops remained stationed in the country until 1956. The term "independence within the French Union" translated to outward signs of independence, such as the issuance of Laotian, Vietnamese, Cambodian stamps, and foreign diplomatic recognition; but French influence was still dominant.

Yet Indochina in 1946 was very different from Indochina in 1939. The Vietnamese, Laotians and Cambodians had seen a French administration bowing to Japanese demands; many had learned of the ideas of Communism, many had learned how to use modern weapons, and most of all, the Viet Minh was a well organized resistance organization.

Military resistance increased; the French, unwilling to give up their colonial Empire, also stepped up their military efforts. In 1954, the French lost the decisive Battle of Dien Bien Phu. The subsequent treaty negotiations at Geneva split Vietnam along the latitude known as the 17th parallel and called for nationwide elections for reunification to be held in 1956.

Surprisingly, after the Viet Minh victory at Dien Bien Phu, there was little spontaneous backlash against the tangible mementos of French domination. Cities, towns, streets and municipal buildings were re-named, statues and monuments removed, but there was no attempt to destroy the most obvious symbols of colonialism, the many pseudo-French public buildings, chateaus and hill stations. The new Vietnamese authorities either made use of them for mundane purposes, or left them to rot. Whether this policy was by design or default, the result was that many are still standing.

For more photos, links to internet sites and other information regarding the subjects in this book, go to the authors blog at http://maka189.wordpress.com

Appendices A – Combat Reports

Sank 1 x 400' freighter and probably sank 1 x 450' freighter (1 B-24 missing) HEADQUARTERS FOURTEENTH U.S. AIR FORCE KUNMING, CHINA. *WEEKLY INTELLIGENCE SUMMARY FOR PERIOD ENDING 3 JANUARY 1945.*

COMPLETE USAAF POST COMBAT REPORT

SUBJECT: Group Mission Report No. 460, Snooper Strike Mission of the South China Sea and Tonkin Gulf.

TO: Commanding general, Fourteenth Air Force, A.P.O. No. 627.

On the afternoon of 31 December 1944, four (4) LAB B-24s took off from bases in the Kunming area for a Snooper Strike Mission over the waters of the Tonkin Gulf and the South China Sea in the Hainan area. Of the four planes, one turned back early due to mechanical failure, two attacked shipping, sinking 1 x 400 foot transport and probably sinking 1 x 450 foot transport, the fourth plane, No. 782, is missing. The missing plane was last contacted at 0230 hours at which time it was plotted approximately 50 to 60 miles Southwest of Kunming. ***Plane 782 was the Bobcat.***

NOTE: *There is a discrepancy in this Air Force post combat report. The Bobcat could not have been 50 to 60 miles southwest of Kunming at 0230 hours. The town around which all of the crewmen landed, Phu Lang Thuong, was 20 miles northeast of*

Hanoi and over 350 miles from Luliang (roughly 2 hours flying time). If by chance a radio message was received at 0230 hours, it must have been just prior to the crew bailing out and at that time, they were over 300 miles south of base. According to Frank, no radio messages were acknowledged while they were sending their mayday's. It is likely that the report was meant to confuse the Japanese into thinking that the plane had crashed somewhere over the border in China. That way, they wouldn't begin searching for the aircraft wreckage. There was Top Secret electronic gear on board and the Americans wanted to keep the Japanese from finding it.

Plane 453, Lt. Folsom, contacted two vessels (1 x 400 foot transport and 1 x 450 transport [underlined in pencil]) at 17:40 N – 109:20E on a course of 270 degrees; these vessels were within one-half mile of each other. At 2025 hours (local), a run was made on the larger of the two. It was intended only to drop only three bombs but the entire load of eight was accidentally dropped. The bombs were all over on the target vessel, one of them, however, was a near miss on the other vessel.

Plane 443, Lt. Weitz, picked up the same two vessels as those attacked by plane No. 453. They were picked up on the radar screen at about the same time that a radio message telling their location was received from plane No. 453. One run was made on the large of the two vessels at 2125 hours (local). Three bombs were dropped at intervals of 50 feet from 600 feet altitude, the run being from 2 o'clock. One bomb was a direct hit.[underlined in pencil] Due to the bombay doors refusing to open, the second run was not made until an hour later. In approaching, it was seen that the two vessels had stopped moving and were parallel to each other about twenty feet apart. Seven bombs were dropped on this run from 1,000 feet altitude across the beam of the two vessels. A second direct hit was inflicted on the vessel originally attacked; it had been smoking and now burst into flames. Two direct hits were scored [underlined in pencil] on the second vessel, the interval between bombs being 50 feet; this vessel was seen to explode. Claim 1 x 400 foot transport sunk, and 1 x 450 foot transport probably sunk. [underlined in pencil]

Plane 782 was shot down at PHU LANG THUONG. Of the 11 men of the crew 8 were recovered by the French. Cared for in three groups, they passed successively the frontier in three different places. The remaining 3 men are missing.

An aircraft piloted by Lt. R.W. Smith ran into difficulty after being hit by AA fire in a bombing attack against enemy shipping on January 1. The crew bailed out in FIC. Fortunately the majority of the crew members though the help of a super secret organization made their homeward way successfully. Those mission and believed either captured by the enemy or dead are:

Pilot	Robert W. Smith, Lieutenant
Co-Pilot	Frank. D. Padgett, Lieutenant
Navigator	Everett A. Clark, Lieutenant
Bombardier	Harry W. Sherer, Lieutenant
Radio Operator	Stanley J. Brach, Sergeant
Radar Operator	Joseph P. Medon, Sergeant
Engineer	William Gottschall, Sergeant
Nose Gunner	Hugh C. Pope, Staff Sergeant
Top Turret Gunner	George Uhrine, Sergeant
Ball Turret Gunner	John J. Webster, Corporal
Tail Gunner	Will D. Sanderson, Sergeant

JOHN G. ARMSTRONG,

Colonel, Air Corps,
Commanding

Appendices B - War Crimes Trial Manuscript

WAR CRIMES TRIAL: NICKS & DEMARIA
MARCH-JUN 1946

"Americans Beheaded After Saigon Bombing Attempt," THE STRAITS TIMES, Friday, March 29, 1946

On June 12, 1945 a United States Army B-24 bomber of the 380th (H) Bomb Group, 529th Squadron, Philippines, crashed about 30 kilometers from Cholon, FI-C. The only two known American survivors of the crash were taken to the Kempeitai prison in Saigon and incarcerated.

About three weeks later the two Americans were placed in an automobile with some Japanese Kempeis (Kempeitai men), and driven to a secluded spot near an airfield, where both men were beheaded. The bodies were hurriedly covered with earth, and the spot covered with a cut tire. The Japanese then returned to Saigon.

Yesterday [March 28th, 1946], in Singapore's War Crimes Court before Lieut. Col. L.G. Coleman, in the first case in Singapore relating to Japanese outrages against Americans, First Lieut. J.W. Sands leveled a charge against W/O Tomono Shundo of the Saigon Kempeitai, of being concerned in the killing of the two American airmen.

In a short opening address, Lieut. Sands said that the crime he was about to describe was not only a flagrant violation of the universally accepted and admitted laws of war, but it also constituted a violation of the tenets of humanity and chivalry upon which the laws of war are founded.

Lieut. Sands then proceeded to outline what the prosecution intended to prove in the case. He said that on June 12 last year an American bomber on a mission from the Philippines to bomb the railway at Saigon crashed about 30 kilometers from Cholon.

The only two known American survivors of the crash, Allen Nicks and Joseph Demaria, were taken to the Kempeitai prison in Saigon, and incarcerated. On a day early in July, W/O Tomono, the accused, ordered Iyoki Kazuyoshi to accompany him on a special assignment. This order was likewise given to L/Cpl. Kawai Yoshio and Sgt. Okomoto Yoshima.

Tomono then ordered Kawai and Okomoto to bring the two American prisoners from their place of confinement to the rear of the buildings. Kawai and Okomoto bound the hands of Nicks and Demaria and, at the direction of Tomono, brought them out without shoes.

BEHEADED NEAR AIRFIELD

The two Americans were placed in a car with Tomono, Kawai, Okomoto, Iyoki, and another Japanese, Arai. The vehicle was driven to a secluded spot at or near Kong [sic: Long] Thanh airfield, Arai driving and Tomono directing the route.

Tomono and Arai went into a secluded spot in the woods and Tomono, a short time later, ordered Kawai to bring Nicks, the smaller of the two Americans. He was taken to a spot where Tomono and Arai were standing, and where there was a hole in the ground already prepared. Tomono compelled the American to kneel down on a pile of dirt beside the hold and, having assured himself that no one was watching, struck the American on the back of the head with a sword, almost but not completely severing the head from the body. The American died immediately, and his body rolled into the hole in the ground.

Tomono then ordered Okomoto to bring the other American (DeMaria) from the vehicle to the same spot. The process was repeated, except that this time Arai wielded the sword and completely decapitated the American. Arai had subsequently committed suicide on Oct. 10 last year when about to be arrested by the British.

"The usual Japanese defense [sic] that the orders to kill came from military superiors is anticipated," said Lieut. Sands. "But on this score, it is again pointed out that this was a crime against the laws of humanity and that such an order, even if given, was an illegal order."

NO JUSTIFICATION

"No justification for the killings of Nicks or Demaria has ever been shown. In fact, Tomono, the accused, has unequivocally admitted that the two Americans received no trial or hearing whatsoever."

Lieut. Sands also brought to the attention of the court the fact that all the other Japanese military and Kempeitai personnel concerned in the killing are being held by the French authorities at Saigon for other serious crimes against French subjects or nationals and would be brought to justice in due time by the French.

As the prosecution's supporting evidence, Lieut. Sands produced a number of affidavits made by Japanese Kempeis concerned in the case, and also statements made by French nationals and subjects who were at one time or another, confined together with the American aviators.

After the prosecution case had been closed, Japanese defense counsel applied for an adjournment on the grounds that three witnesses important to the defense case had not yet arrived in Singapore from Saigon. The applications was granted and the case adjourned till Monday morning.

Tomono Shundo, Japanese Kempeitai warrant officer from Saigon and alleged killer of one of American airmen who parachuted from a crashing B-24 west of Saigon in June last year, spoke with feeling of an admonition from his father and related a story of a sick family cat in making his defense in Singapore's First War Crimes Court yesterday [1 April 1946].

First Lieut. J.W. Sands, American prosecuting officer, interrupted Tomono's reminiscences on the grounds that he was being irrelevant, but he President, Lieut. Col. L.G. Coleman, smilingly remarked: "I don't think that what he is saying is relevant, but I would not say it is strictly irrelevant."

Tomono, who stands charged with being concerned in the killing of the American aviators, Technical Sergeants Allen W. Nicks and Joseph A. Demaria, admitted that he was present at the execution, but denied that he beheaded either of the American. "I was cutting down branches while Arai (who has since committed suicide) beheaded the Americans," he said.

The trial which started on Thursday last week was continued yesterday with Tomono in the witness box all day. At the request of his defense [sic] counsel, Tomono told a rambling story of the events which led up to the beheading of the American airmen.

He said that either on the third or fourth Saturday in June last year, Capt. Hisakwa, chief of his sub-section in the Saigon Kempeitai, told him that it had been decided to execute the Americans, and that he, Tomono, was to carry out the execution.

"When I was leaving my native place in Japan," said Tomono, "my father asked me to refrain from killing any Kempeitai detainees; that if I did no the evil consequences of it would fall on the heads of my wife and children.

"Also in March last year, I received a letter from my wife in which she said that the family cat had been sick, and she had wanted to destroy it, but my father told her not to do so as it would affect her husband's life.

"These memories flashed into my mind when I was ordered to perform the execution, and I was reluctant to do so," said Tomono.

The execution took place on a Sunday afternoon after a Kempeitai banquet. "The two Americans were taken by lorry to a thickly-wooded and seclude spot outside Saigon.

Tomono said that he had decided to shoot the Americans, but on the way Arai had said that it was not favorable [sic] as it would attract notice, and he suggested a Chinese sword which he had brought for the purpose.

When the party arrived at the scene of the execution, Arai and accused led the smaller American (Nicks) to the execution ground, and Arai made him kneel beside a hollow. At this point, Tomono said that, as he did not wish to witness the scene he pretended to cut some branches from nearby trees and in the meantime Arai beheaded the American.

They then fetched the second American, and Arai killed him, too, saying that he did not mind killing another as he had already killed one.

When the Japanese party returned to the lorry, Tomono said that they had to push it 300 meters before it could be started and added, naively: "I told the men the lorry would not start because we had killed the Americans."

Later, in the hands of the prosecutor Sands, Tomono said that the execution had been carried out secretly "because this sort of punishment was an action disgraced to the persons executed, and a public announcement would leave an unpleasant feeling with the people."

Stating that the balance of his mind had been upset by the tortures inflicted on him by the French Investigation Bureau, by whom he had been detained on Dec. 6 Warrant Officer Tomono Shundo, Jap Kempeitai man from Saigon, said in Singapore's First War Crimes Court yesterday that former statements he had made were either wrong or untrue, but that all he had said in court was the truth.

Tomono, who is standing trail on a charge of being concerned in the killing of two American aviators in Saigon in July last year, again denied that he had beheaded one of them. He said that he had supervised the execution on orders from his superiors, but not before he had first tried to avoid carrying out the order.

President: As I understand it, an order given by a superior officer in the Japanese Army emanates from the Emperor and, therefore, is sacred?

-- Yes.

President: And it would be unthinkable to disobey such an order?

-- Yes, but I submitted the opinion that the execution be carried out by the Police section and not by my section.

President: Now, having submitted your opinion, what was the reply you received?

-- My submission was rejected.

President: So you were ordered to carry out the execution?

-- Yes.

President: Then why didn't you execute the prisoners yourself?

-- I was ordered to execute, but it did not mean by that I had to execute them myself.

President: You know that one or more of your subordinates have said that you did execute one of the Americans?

-- It was there mistake.

President: Yesterday you said that they may have had a grudge against you because you were too much of a disciplinarian.

-- Yes.

President: Didn't you think that if they had a grudge against you, they would have said you committed both executions and not merely one?

-- I don't know what the NCOs were thinking, but under the torture inflicted on them and the clever leading questions put to them, they may have been confused and answered incorrectly.

President: You think that the interrogators were clever enough to make the NCOs admit you killed one man and that they were not clever enough to make them admit you killed both?

-- I think that way.

President: When were you tortured in Saigon?

-- Since Dec. 6, the day I was detained, I was tortured for one week.

President: Did you tell that to the United States and British officers who questioned you?

-- No.

President: Not a word about you being tortured?

-- Yes.

President: You did not tell the American officer that he must not mind what you were saying because your mind was ricketty [sic] with torture?

-- No.

President: Why did you bring a Chinese sword to the execution?

-- When I left the cells for the execution I did not know it existed, but I was told later.

Tomono went on to state that Arai who, he said, beheaded both Americans and had since committed suicide, was a man of very big physique and what he did was most extraordinary.

He said that he did not question Arai when he saw the sword, as he had a deep respect for Arai who, within a few months, was to have been promoted to the rank of warrant officer. Arai had beheaded the Americans without asking Tomono's permission and while his back was turned.

President: You were in charge of the party?

-- Yes.

President: You were not much of a disciplinarian then, were you?

--Now that I come to think of it, that is so.

President: Not likely, then, that anyone would have a grudge against you if you were not a disciplinarian.

-- I was very strict in carrying out army orders.

In reply to further questions, Tomono said that he did not think beheading was worse than shooting so he did not reprimand Arai for bring a sword, although he (Tomono), had ordered one of the NCOs to bring pistols. He said that he bore no grudge against the Americans, but carried out the execution, although he was reluctant to do so, because he had thought the order he had received was lawful.

At this stage, 11:30 yesterday morning, the court was adjourned till two o'clock to enable the defense to call three witnesses from Saigon who had already arrived in Singapore Roads. It was however, 3:45 p.m. before the witnesses finally did arrive, and Cpl. Takano, from the Saigon Kempeitai, was immediately called to the box.

Referring to the execution of the Americans, he said that Tomono and Arai and three others had formed the execution party. He said, he firmly believed Tomono acted under orders from Major Tomida.

263

Tomono Shundo, Jap Kempei from Saigon who, after the execution of two Americans, said "As I have killed many men, when I die – it will be a painful death," was yesterday sentenced to death by hanging in Singapore's First War Crimes Court.

Thus, after four days' hearing, ended the first war crimes trial in South East Asia in which an American prosecutor, on behalf of American prosecutor, on behalf of American victims of the Japanese, appeared in a court of British officers.

Lieut. Col. L.G. Coleman, President of the Court, congratulated First Lieut. J.W. Sands, the prosecutor, on the fair and restrained manner in which he had presented his case, and added that it was a great pleasure to the Court that the whole trial had been conducted with such naturalness. Earlier, the President had also congratulated the Japanese defense counsel, Mr. Doi, on the admirable and striking manner in which he had conducted the defense.

Tomono, who had been found guilty of being concerned in the killing of two American aviators. Technical Sergeants Allen W. Nicks and Joseph A. Demaria, in Saigon in July last year, had said that, although he had supervised the execution, under orders, he had not actually beheaded either of the Americans.

But when the court returned to announce the verdict, the President told him: "You have been found guilty of a crime as horrible as any disclosed in this Court. You robbed two gallant airmen of their lives in such a manner as to send a shudder through the civilized world. You did not accord these men the slightest degree of clemency.

"There can be only one penalty for you. You shall die. The sentence of this Court, subject to confirmation, is that you suffer death by hanging."

In his final address, Lieut. Sands had asked the Court for a deterrent punishment. "It is clearly undeniable," he said, "that Tomono is a smart, shrewd and calculating operator. He tries to leave nothing to chance. He carried into his statement and into this Court the same sly methods he used to kill.

"We ask that the punishment imposed, if the Court finds this man guilty, be of such a kind that it will carry a deterrent effect sufficient to insure that future civilizations will not be burdened with such barbarians.

"At the outset, the prosecution stated the only punishment that could hope to atone for this crime was death by hanging. We now prefer to conclude our statement with the suggestion to the Court that Tomono select his own punishment if found guilty. He had selected it. He selected it on that fateful day at Long Thanh in July 1943 when he said, "As I have killed many men, when I die it will be a painful death."

Pleading for the prisoner, the Japanese counsel, both in his final address and in mitigation, submitted that the execution had been carried out in accordance with orders from a superior officer, and that the accused had thought the order was lawful.

Appendices C - The Story of Ensigns Quinn and Grady

The following account is from the website vpnavy.com.

Crew Eight of VPB-25 had already logged 35 missions when disaster struck on January 26, 1945, following a forced landing off the coast of French Indochina near Vung Tau. The crew salvaged all possible gear from their sinking PBM, paddled ashore in a raft and hurried into the jungle. Thus began a valiant three month saga of escape and evasion to elude Japanese troops.

The rescue plan for Crew Eight included evacuation by submarine from the vicinity of Sa Huyhn. Only one man was successfully removed via an Australian sub, aboard which he stayed for a full combat tour. During the rescue, the sub sweated out more than 100 depth charge explosions. Enemy advances precluded further rescue attempts by submarine.

Crew Eight, now in the hands of a French underground unit, was moved regularly to various locations in the country. They were joined by a pilot who had been shot down on January 12, flying from the aircraft carrier Essex. A new plan for their evacuation was formulated. The plan was to evacuate the crew by air. However, their situation deteriorated badly when the Japanese overthrew the French on March 9. French citizens were to be rounded up for imprisonment.

The group of flyers broke into two groups and went separate ways. A Frenchman named Trocoire, part of the French underground unit, took the two PBM pilots and the pilot from the Essex north into Montegnard country, stopping at Ple Tonal, 60 miles from Tourane (Danang).
On April 8, they departed for Hue to arrange sea evacuation. Tragically, they were captured and killed. The circumstances of their deaths remain unknown but it was rumored they were buried alive.

The other group of men from the PBM joined a couple of French resistance fighters who supplied them weapons and ammunition. On April 27, they were betrayed by an Indochinese sergeant and ambushed by a Japanese platoon. The men fought the superior forces until they ran out of ammunition. They were captured and for resisting the Japanese, seven of the crew were executed gangland style, shot in the back of the head while kneeling, their hands and arms tied behind their backs. The dead were eventually interred in a common grave in India.

END

Appendices D - Otto Schwartz Story

The following excerpt is from an account written by Otto Schwarz, one of the American prisoners in the British, Dutch and American camp.

"We arrived in Saigon in early April of 1944 and were taken to a camp on Rue Jean Eudel, which is along the river at the docks in the southern end of Saigon.... Around the beginning of September of 1945, I believe about the fifth, an American Capt., I do not know if he was Air Force or Army, came to the main gate and entered the camp and wanted an accounting of the Americans. There were 198 Americans in the camp. The next day we left the camp and we were finally liberated on September 6, 1945, my 22nd birthday. We were taken to the airport where there were 6 C-47's, which we boarded, and I had my first airplane ride."

"We left Saigon and flew to Karachi, India where we boarded C-47's. From there we were flown to Calcutta to an American Army Hospital. We remained at the hospital, which was the 142nd General Hospital, for a short period of time. There we were issued uniforms of Army khaki, and were given $100 advance pay and allowed to go into Calcutta as free men. For the first time in almost 4 years we were allowed to roam around as free men and do anything we wanted and buy anything we wanted; what an experience it was for us. After our short stay at the 142nd General

Hospital, we were placed on aircraft and flown across India, North Africa, south Atlantic into Bermuda. From Bermuda into Washington, D.C. We were finally home and could only thank God that it was all over."

By Otto Schwarz

It is likely that the American captain that Otto Schwarz speaks of coming to the prison gate, was Frank. It may have been difficult for Schwarz to accurately identify his rank as Frank may not have been in uniform. The colonel assigned him that duty and he did as ordered.

Appendices E - Kotohira Jinsha Newspaper Story

First Law Case Wins Fame For Frank Padgett
Vincennes Sun-Commercial, December 4, 1949

EDITOR'S NOTE: Making his first appearance in court after passing the bar examination in Honolulu a few days ago, Frank Padgett, son of David H. and Mrs. Eva M. Padgett, of Vincennes, Indiana, scored over government attorneys in such a fashion that the Associated Press carried this story, going out to all parts of the world.

HONOLULU-(AP)- A young lawyer, in court for the first time, tripped up government attorneys in a legal battle over a Japanese Shinto shrine - and ah, the irony of it.

The lawyer, Frank Padgett, 26, pleading to let the Japanese have their shrine back, spent eight months in a Japanese prison camp during the war. Padgett, a native of Vincennes, Indiana, was shot down over French Indochina in 1945.

The government alien property custodian seized the shrine in wartime on charges that its Japan-born priest had urged emperor worship. Padgett, admitted to the Bar Tuesday, petitioned federal court to restore the shrine.

Government attorneys argued the shrine was controlled by Japanese nationals; that the Shinto creed was a Japanese cult and not a true religion. But they forgot to file a required oath of verification. Padgett caught the omission.

After long argument, Federal Judge J. Frank McLaughlin granted the government time to file a certified document and refused to dismiss the Japanese congregation's suit. After the session, Judge McLaughlin complimented the young attorney for an "excellent job".

Photo Sources

"Aliiolani Hale"	D Ramey Logan 2011
"Free Soup, Coffee."	U.S. National Archives and Records Administration
"Map of San Francisco Worlds Fair"	UC Berkeley Bancroft Library (public
'Harvard"	Harvard College
"Men in Class"	U.S. Air Force Archives
"PT-13"	U.S. Air Force Archives
"BT-14"	U.S. Air Force Archives
"AT-10"	U.S. Air Force Archives
"Langley Field"	U.S. Air Force Archives
"B-24" Production Line"	U.S. Air Force Archives
"Bolivar Jr."	U.S. Air Force Archives
"B-17 Nose Damage"	U.S. Air Force Archives
"LAB B-24 Bomber"	U.S. Air Force Archives
"Ball Turret Damage"	U.S. Air Force Archives
"Crew Photo - Mitchell Field"	Family archive
"The Route"	AJ Padgett
'Waiting for Takeoff"	U.S. Air Force Archives
"Eyes On"	U.S. Air Force Archives
"Cairo"	Public domain
"Street Scene"	Public domain
"Karachi"	Public domain
"Taj Mahal"	U.S. Air Force Archives
"Burma Road"	National Museum of the U.S. Air Force
"Trucks on Burma Road"	U.S. Air Force Archives
"Chabua Airfield"	U.S. Air Force Archives
"The Hump"	Public domain
"In China"	Family archive
"Runway Work"	United States Army Air Force via National Archives
"P-40's"	United States Army Air Force via National Archives
"Luliang Village"	Public domain
"Map"	Public domain
"Bombs Away"	U.S. Air Force Archives

"Maintenance Crew"	U.S. Air Force Archives
"B-24 Cockpit"	U.S. Air Force Archives
"Paddies"	Public domain
"Kempeitai"	Public domain
"Kempeitai Train"	Showa History Vol.7: February 26 Incident
"Wrecked Bridge"	U.S. Air Force Archives
"B-25 Strafing"	U.S. Air Force Archives, collection of Jack Heyn
"Court Scene"	Honolulu Advertiser

QUELQUES BOURREAUX	Copyright G.H.B., Saigon 1947
RECEPTION	Copyright G.H.B., Saigon 1947
LE NOUVEAU	Copyright G.H.B., Saigon 1947
DEPART POUR L'INTERROGATOIRE	Copyright G.H.B., Saigon 1947
PATURE	Copyright G.H.B., Saigon 1947
OTIA!	Copyright G.H.B., Saigon 1947
REVES	Copyright G.H.B., Saigon 1947
AVEUX SPONTANES	Copyright G.H.B., Saigon 1947
DIS LA VERITE	Copyright G.H.B., Saigon 1947
UNE SUITE D'INTERROGATOIRE	Copyright G.H.B., Saigon 1947

The copyrighted illustrations depicting the conditions of prisoners in Kempeitai jails are taken from a book published in Saigon in 1947 by Imprimerie Française d'Outre Mer. The book was sent to Frank by a group of Frenchmen (G.H.B.) who had been imprisoned and tortured in the Kempeitai jails around French Indochina in World War Two. Frank personally knew many of them. These images are perhaps the only representations of what happened in the Kempeitai jails in French Indochina.

All photo's marked U.S. Air Force Archives are the works of a U.S. Air Force Airman or employee, taken or made during the course of the

person's official duties. As a work of the U.S. federal government, the
*image or file is in the **public domain**.*

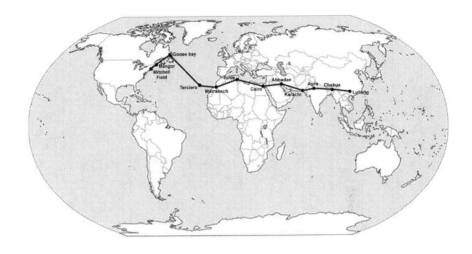

Made in the USA
Lexington, KY
03 June 2015